Timber Fences

Edgar (Ted) Stubbersfield

CONTENTS

ABBREVIATIONS

CCA	Copper, Chrome and Arsenic
CHH	Carter Holt Harvey
HDG	Hot Dipped Galvanised
JIT	Just in time
LOSP	Light Organic Solvent Preservative
PAA	Plywood Association of Australia
RTA	Roads and Traffic Authority
VPI	Vacuum Pressure Impregnated

ACKNOWLEDGMENTS

In preparing this guide to timber fences I was greatly assisted by the following people:

Ralph Bailey
Principal Architect, Guymer Bailey Architects

Dennis and Carole Clark

Rhett Faithfull
Owner, Muckert's Sawmill

Claus Jehne
Principal, Japancom.

Norm Keighron
Director, Keighron Fencing Ltd, UK.

Aki Kurata
CEO, Kurata Co. Ltd.

Graeme Lavuschewski
Owner, Westside Timbers

Colin MacKenzie,
Technical Consultant, Timber Queensland.

Bill Thorn
Parkside Timbers

Errol Wildman

Glen Wilson
Owner, Injune Cypress

INTRODUCTION

Fig. 1. A fence can be more than just a barrier.

Good fences may make for good neighbours, but they can be much more than that. In their form they can be an architectural statement giving character to a property and reflect the personality of the owner. With a very limited range of basic products a great variety of styles[1] can be constructed. A fence can be a very expensive cast and wrought iron barrier requiring very skilled artisans through to brick and on to simple, low cost paling fences that can be built by most handymen. Fences can reflect the high degree of skill possessed by an architect as seen in Figure One or can be, to not put too fine a point on it, an eyesore and completely out of character with an area.

Fig. 2. A fence can also be an eyesore.

---

[1] One fencing group, All Day Fencing, maintains they have over 400 fence designs.
http://www.alldayfencing.com.au/adfproduct0807.php.

But regardless of their multitude of forms, they must fulfil the purpose for which they are intended which can include:

- defining property boundaries
- providing privacy and screening
- providing security
- providing acoustic separation i.e. along freeways etc
- providing children or animal separation or exclusion i.e. from neighbours, from roads, from swimming pools etc, and
- give character and improved aesthetics to a property.

When planning a fence it is important that you have a clear understanding of what the outcome should be.

Fig. 3. Australian hardwood fence Tokushima, Japan

Form and function can sometimes be in tension. Some time ago I supplied a timber fence to Japan. It had a beautiful, simple form for which the Japanese are renowned and I asked for images of it installed to add to my "brag sheet". Expecting to see the fence gracing a park, I was horrified to see it used as traffic barrier. In a collision, the rails may well have speared the driver and the drop on the other side would have ensured a minor accident was potentially fatal. It failed dismally is its function. An unsightly Armco style barrier was what was needed.

This book is not primarily concerned with what might be called "utility fencing" as may be used in a domestic fence where the owner is quite happy with a 15 year life and then move on to the next fad of design. The contents of this book are intended for professionals who are accountable to clients in commercial projects and require repeatability of quality from project to project. The more discerning residential customer who wishes to go beyond utility fencing will also find this guide helpful.

This guide to timber fences is not primarily concerned with helping you design an architectural masterpiece or give a deep understanding of the different functions. Design professionals should already have a good understanding of both form and function. The aim of this book is initially to help you design what you have in mind through incorporating best practice in detailing. The guide will then assist you in specifying the material correctly and then have it built with best practice in construction. Note that I did not say, "Best practice in supply". This is because, for domestic fencing at least, the materials are so inexpensive that there will be compromises in timber quality. This book will help you make informed choices regarding quality and durability. The book will conclude with some thoughts on how to improve the basic paling fence.

1. THE BASICS

There is a myriad of fence styles and it is impossible to say that there is one ideal fence; this is completely a matter of whether the fence meets its intended purpose. We can though, speak authoritatively about good and bad construction and supply. Construction methods vary considerably across the country and here there definitely are bad practices. These, such as setting hardwood posts in concrete, should not come as great revelations as they are spoken against in timber industry entry level documentation. Despite this, most professional fence builders seem to be unaware of them.

Supply of suitable material also can appear to confound some. It is quite simple. Weather exposed timber, particularly timber that is installed in the ground, has to be durable. Subsequent chapters will take you through what you need to know. It is all very logical.

Because the most commonly used fence is the paling fence, the bulk of this book relates to it. The terminology used throughout this book is as follows:

Capping	A board along the top of the fence, generally profiled to shed moisture and slotted on the underside to accept the palings.
Paling	A thin section timber facing to the timber frame, frequently 100 mm wide and from 12 to 25 mm thick.
Picket	A short paling available with different top profiles.
Post	The vertical member that supports the rails. They can be either end or intermediate.
Top Rail	The uppermost horizontal member running between the posts
Middle Rail	The middle horizontal member running between the posts
Bottom Rail	The lowest horizontal member running between the posts
Plinth	A timber board that fills any gap between the ground and the palings
Bay Width	The distance between the posts, also called "post spacing"

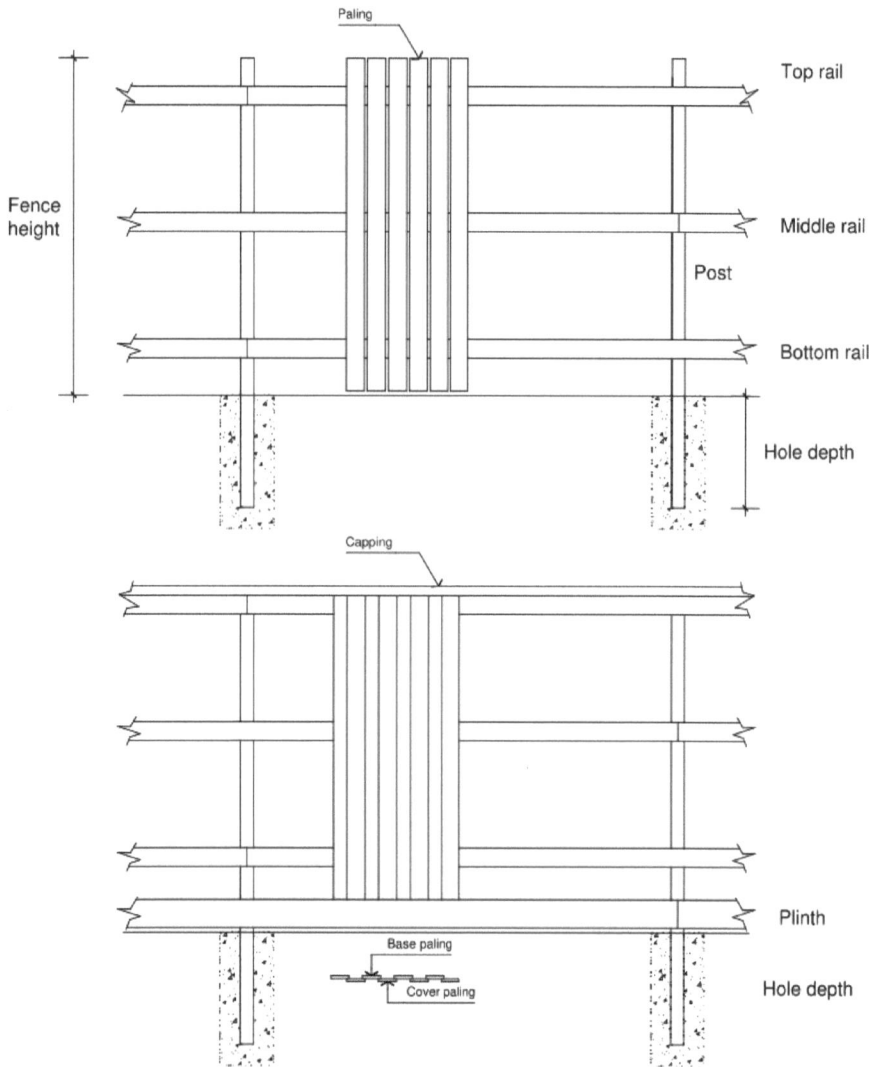

Fig. 4. Illustration of terminology.

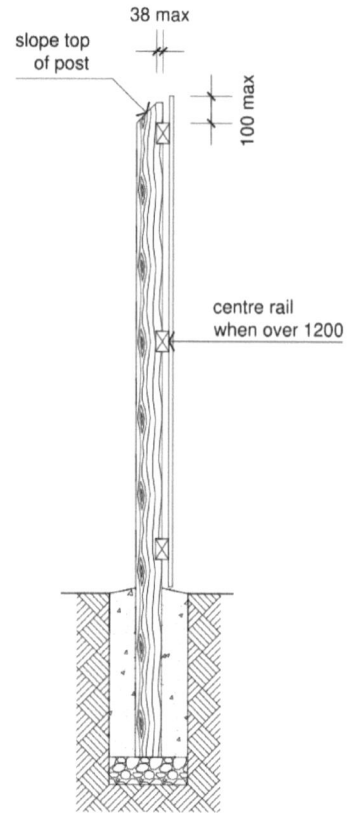

Fig. 5. Basic fence layout.

The one basic frame design allows for a variety of fence types to be constructed on that frame. It will allow for battens to be installed vertically or aligned diagonally. It will also allow for the palings to be dispensed with altogether and replaced with sheeting which could be ply or roofing iron. Using the very best of material is not enough. You must give attention to very basic detailing but this will be rewarded by having a fence that ages gracefully. None of this detailing is complicated and includes such simple measures as sloping (or capping) the top of the posts and ensuring that the palings do not touch or be embedded in the ground.

Fig. 6. Consider the wisdom of checking out the post.

Figure Five shows a maximum of 38 mm check into the post which is common practice and this practice is too ingrained to change but, despite that, it probably should be reviewed. A 100x75 mm post is reduced to 62x75 mm and I have seen hardwood posts checked this deeply snap at groundline in heavy winds (Figure Six). Perhaps 12 mm should be the maximum. With stainless steel batten screws, the need for checking is done away with entirely. Alternately a slightly more complex construction where the rails fit between the posts could be adopted.

2. TIMBER SPECIES AND QUALITY

Imported timber is generally too expensive[2] to be used in fencing so we are normally dealing with Australian produced material. The timbers used can be plantation pine, cypress or hardwood, each with its advantages and disadvantages. A potential purchaser of fencing material has no problem seeing advertisements for quality, top quality or even premium quality fencing material. But the advertising claims and the reality can be widely divergent. The sad reality is that there are no standards for fencing materials so what is considered suitable and what is considered "quality" varies with the supplier and the reseller as it does with installer and end customer. In the absence of written standards, who is the arbiter of what is acceptable?

To understand the issue of quality in regards to fencing, consider the most visible part - the paling and how it is generally produced. The pine logs used for palings will typically be the much smaller and lower value first thinning. Often they are a relatively even size. They are docked to length and then fed into a twin saw which cuts the billet into a piece with two opposing faces at 100 mm (or 75 mm) apart. The billet is laid down on one of the flat sides and then passed through a multi-rip saw. The outer pieces with the natural round are discarded and the resultant block of palings is stacked ready for treating. All this can be fully automated. It is important to understand that not one of the stacked palings has been inspected so, to talk of "quality", is misleading. The price paid for the product is so low that there is no room for quality inspection or any step that might reduce the recovery or slow production. The situation can be much the same with the pine posts and it would be unusual for them to be structurally graded.[3]

Hardwood palings can be very different. They were traditionally cut individually as fall-down sizes and only produced when the timber billet going through the mill had reduced to the point that structural timber or 25 mm boards could not be recovered. These went through the normal docking process and at least some inspection was done but, in the absence of standards, this was prone to be very subjective. Alternatively, "optional"[4] logs were directed to landscaping and fencing but still had the same cutting and grading process. There are some mills that just produce landscaping material and hardwood palings can be block cut without grading like the pine palings. Because of the high quality of the paling that are produced at some mills, the variation in quality between palings from different hardwood producers is probably much more than with pine.

Cypress palings are cut in much the same way as hardwood. They are primarily cut as a recovery line, rather than a first cut and, like hardwood, go under visual grading prior to docking.[5] A similar comment about quality variation would apply.

For a normal domestic fence purchased from a reseller, you must expect that the timber will contain

---

[2] One company's online quote tool gave an installed price of $1,650 for a basic 30 m long treated 1.8m pine paling fence with cypress posts compared to $5,850 for a similar fence in merbau – date visited Dec 28, 2015.

[3] As an example, *Ironwood*, a treated pine landscaping timber, with some sizes incised, manufactured by CCH is described as "Not Suitable for structural applications e.g. structural retaining walls."
http://www.chhwoodproducts.com.au/ironwoodlandscaping/ Date visited 8 October 2015.

[4] Optional logs are those that are considered too low grade to use to cut framing or are shorter than 2.4m. They had, in the past, been sold at a very reduced royalty but extraction and milling costs were basically the same so the savings were not as may be expected.

[5] Wilson, Glen. *Pers. Com.* October 12, 2015.Glen is the owner/manager of Injune Cypress.

natural features such as knots, gum veins, minor insect damage, want, wane, etc. You may even experience some cupping and twisting etc. This is all to be expected of a low priced (at least to the producer) timber product. For domestic fence applications this is generally acceptable. But individual residential clients can have a much greater expectation of quality and almost certainly this will be the case with commercial projects. In these cases a higher quality product should be ordered.

Timber Queensland specification advice on grades is generally sound. This is:

Posts and railings: structurally graded timber (e.g. cypress F5, hardwood F11, treated pine F5 or MGP10)

Palings: the following limitations could be specified in all species: no loose or unsound knots, no decay or insect galleries, no heart or pith gum, latex or resin pockets not to extend from one surface to another, sound knots not to exceed 50% of face width. [6]

Our suggestion would be to accept the Timber Queensland specification but upgrade the hardwood posts to F14[7] (of appropriate species) and specifically mention heart free and also limit the knots in palings to 40% of the face. Alternatively, accept the Timber Queensland specification and over order by 5 – 10% and cull on site. It must be appreciated that producing material to higher quality will mean that the cost is higher than normal domestic grade. The mill may charge the same rates that they do for structural timber.[8] A suitable specification is critical for commercial projects where the sometimes lower quality domestic fencing would be completely unacceptable. Refer to the chapter on commercial fencing for guidance on larger section size "designer" fences.

Preservation

Because the timber is generally unseasoned, alternatives to VPI waterborne preservatives such as LOSP cannot be used. But because of the need to use the most economical treatment possible, these alternatives also would not be used as they are more expensive. Treatments used will be waterborne and frequently CCA is still used, particularly for pine. The response to treatment varies dramatically depending on the type of timber used.

---

[6] Timber Queensland. *Technical Data Sheet 20, Residential Timber Fences*. (Brisbane: Timber Queensland. 2014) 1.

[7] Refer to Appendix 1 of my book, *Grading Hardwood*, where the visual acceptability of F11 hardwood is discussed as opposed to its structural adequacy.

[8] A high quality hardwood paling, 100x16 mm x 1.8m cut especially at $1100 per m3 will cost $3.17 (before a merchant's profit) compared to a "big box" retailer price of $1.23 for the same size in treated pine (October 2015). GST is extra.

Fig. 7. Incised pine.

Fig. 8. Decay in non incised pine

Pine: The sapwood of pine readily accepts preservatives but the heart cannot be penetrated using standard methods. Fortunately, the first cut thinning are almost all sapwood so this presents little problem. Heartwood should be limited to no more than 20%. This is seldom an issue with the palings but can be an issue with the posts, particularly if they are cut from second cut thinning or final cut logs where the heartwood content is much larger. The only way correct treatment of the posts can be ensured is by incising[9] to a depth of 8 mm. It is important to specify the depth of the incision and to require a conformance check on site.[10] Because of cost, CCA is frequently used as the preservative.[11] Pine should be preconditioned, normally by steam, prior to treatment to ensure the best outcome but this is not always done due to cost and it is not possible to tell preconditioned from non preconditioned treated pine. Requiring certificates would be prudent.

Treatment will not make the timber stable and, in the harsher Queensland weather, pine palings can twist and warp so badly that an owner might reasonably expect to replace the palings every 10 years. In Victoria, the same product will perform very differently.

Fig. 9. Sapwood band on spotted gum.

Fig. 10. Pack of CCA treated hardwood (green) in between Tanalith E/ACQ (brown) treated palings.

Hardwood: The sapwood band can be very broad on some species such as spotted gum but on others it can be very narrow. Ironbark and blackbutt are examples of species with a much narrower sapwood boundary. The amount of sapwood that will take preservative in individual pieces could vary from almost 100% to nothing. This would be a major concern with pine but, because of the natural durability of many hardwood species, it is not a concern when they are used. Because there is only a small uptake of chemical with hardwood and the convenience of having the framing and palings treated at the same plant, hardwood palings are now normally treated with non chrome, non arsenic chemicals.

A number of common species contain starch in their sapwood making them susceptible to Lyctus attack which will reduce the sapwood to powder long before it would have decayed.

Cypress: It is impossible to treat Cypress sapwood with waterborne preservatives. If kiln dried, the timber has been successfully treated with LOSP (up to 19 mm thick) but cost is going to preclude this for fencing. So, theoretically, a paling containing cypress sapwood should not be durable but they have proven to last far longer than reason would normally dictate. Being a thin cross section, they dry very quickly after becoming wet and moisture is required for the timber to decay. The sapwood is not eaten by lyctus which would be an issue with many untreated hardwood products. As for the posts they should be able to be purchased with minimal sapwood (up to 20% is acceptable).[13] While the natural durability has been dropped from In Ground 1 to In Ground 2, it is at the

Fig. 11. Tops of 30 year old cypress palings in Brisbane[12]

high end of the lower grouping. So long as the posts are not set in concrete cypress will perform extremely well and give a preservative free option for places like childcare centres.

Cypress marketing often points out its naturally termite resistance (many hardwoods are as well) and it is usually only attacked when the fibres are breaking down. Whereas pine and hardwood palings are usually only 16 mm thick, cypress is usually sold as an ex 25 mm product. In the southern market particularly these palings are sold with "Windsor" tops. This improves the quality as inferior timber is removed during processing as it can cause problems going through the picketing machine.

---

[12] Mackenzie, Colin. "My 30 year old cypress fence. Very little decay in palings (mainly weathering) and not much in rails either. Even untreated sappy pine or cypress or hardwood palings tend not to rot as sections so thin and they dry out too quick after they become wet. Run Timberlife software and you will see what I mean." *Pers. Com.* Oct 14, 2015.

[13] Wildman, Errol. "Attempts were made to limit the sapwood in palings but it proved impractical". *Pers. Com.* 8 December 2015. Errol operated a major cypress sawmill in Wandoan for many years.

3. HARDWOOD – DIGGING DEEPER

While treated pine and cypress can be considered as two largely homogenous groups, the same cannot be said of hardwood, There are over 200 species milled commercially. Some of these, to put not too fine a point on it, are suitable only for packing cases e.g. bloodwood, while others such as Gympie messmate are among the finest hardwoods in the world. The members that make up the fencing also experiences different forms of attack. A paling that dries quickly may only have to primarily counter the effect of UV whereas the post, while having to resist UV, also has to be able to resist decay in ground. As a consequence, a simple specification that just says F11 or F14 hardwood, (a measurement of strength on the day of milling and nothing more) will not address the basic requirements of appearance and durability suitable for the application.

Fig. 12. Hardwood rail decayed after 23 years.

Responsible millers will produce material fit for purpose. The four mills that operated in my home, the Lockyer Valley, could all be relied upon to supply material fit for purpose. All a client had to do was simply ask for "fencing" and, in the background, they took care of the matters that were not understood by the customer. The fence in Figure Twelve is also in the Lockyer Valley but in this case the builder sublet the fence construction to a fencing contractor from "out of town" who did not purchase from any of those four mills. The rails appear to be either rose gum or Sydney blue gum, both In Ground 3 and Above Ground 2 species. They have failed badly, the posts also have rotted off. Of the four mills I referred to, only one is still in operation and it no longer cuts fencing[14] so local purchasers only have access to product sold through landscaping yards etc. It is critical that the purchaser/specifier be in charge of the specification and not trust to something vague like "hardwood fencing".

---

[14] Faithful, Rhett. "We don't supply any fencing contractors as we don't cut any fencing grade….there's no money in it. Most of the contractors around here get their fencing grade material with heart in 4 x 4's and needless to say they are rubbish". *Pers. Com.* November 19, 2015.

Fig. 13. Hardwood posts with heart in the centre

Fig. 14. Better quality posts – only two out of 56 contain significant amount of heart.

For jobs where there is a higher expectation and, a basic expectation of quality, there should be no heart (or pith) in the timber. Testing has shown that the timber is structurally sound in some species if it is fully contained (which it seldom is in smaller fencing sizes e.g. 100x100 mm). This is why it was permitted in the 2007 edition of AS2082 Timber - Hardwood - Visually stress-graded for structural purposes. But that standard recognises that there are issues with this quality timber and says, "The allowance [of heart] only relates to the primary structural properties of the timber. For applications where appearance or other serviceability issues are important, it may be appropriate to restrict inclusion of heart, pith and heart shakes".[15]

Posts should always be a Durability 1 In Ground species with shrinkage limited to a maximum of 7%. Some Species in this group include forest red gum, ironbark and tallowwood. Limiting the shrinkage is important as some Durability One in Ground timbers can have higher shrinkage and exhibit collapse in the process e.g. turpentine shrinkage is 13%. The rails should be at least Durability 1 Above Ground. Species in this group would include spotted gum and blackbutt. Ideally, the palings should be of similar durability so as to avoid replacing the palings while the posts and rails are still in good order.

Readers in Western Australia with access mainly to jarrah (In Ground and Above Ground 2) and karri (In Ground 3 and Above Ground 2) have to take extra care as these species do not have sufficient natural durability to use as posts.[16] In the next chapter I will explain how to add durability to these posts so

---

15 Standards Australia. *AS2082-2010 Visually stress-graded hardwood for structural purposes*. (Standards Australia: Homebush, 2010) 1.4.4.

they will give acceptable performance. Specifying treated to H5 will do nothing to the timber as the chemical only penetrates the sapwood and has no effect on the heartwood, which most, if not all of the post will be.

Fig. 15. Premium Spotted gum used in a fence in Japan

Hardwood, depending on the species selected, will give the greatest potential to build a fence with striking aesthetics but higher grades will need to be specified than would normally be the case for general domestic fencing. Leaching is always an issue with hardwood though may not matter in fences. If leaching is assessed as detrimental, it can be minimised by the use of species with lower tannin content, e.g. spotted gum, and/or through pre-leaching with proprietary products.

---

[16] The Forest Products Commission of Western Australia says of these species "The South West region of Western Australia is home to an array of tree species. The main species used for timber production are jarrah (*Eucalyptus marginata*) and karri (*Eucalyptus diversicolor*) which are renown for their strength and durability." URL: http://www.fpc.wa.gov.au/timbers-our-south-west Date visited: December 16, 2016. Despite the claim of durability these species are not as durable as many found on the east coast where their use would be considered bad practice. An In Ground 3 timber could not be considered durable in an Australia wide setting.

4. INSTALLING TIMBER POSTS

Correctly treated sawn pine posts are straightforward. I have not been made aware of problems associated with setting them in concrete or premix. The preservation chemicals appear to be more effective in pine than hardwood. The same cannot be said of hardwood and cypress.

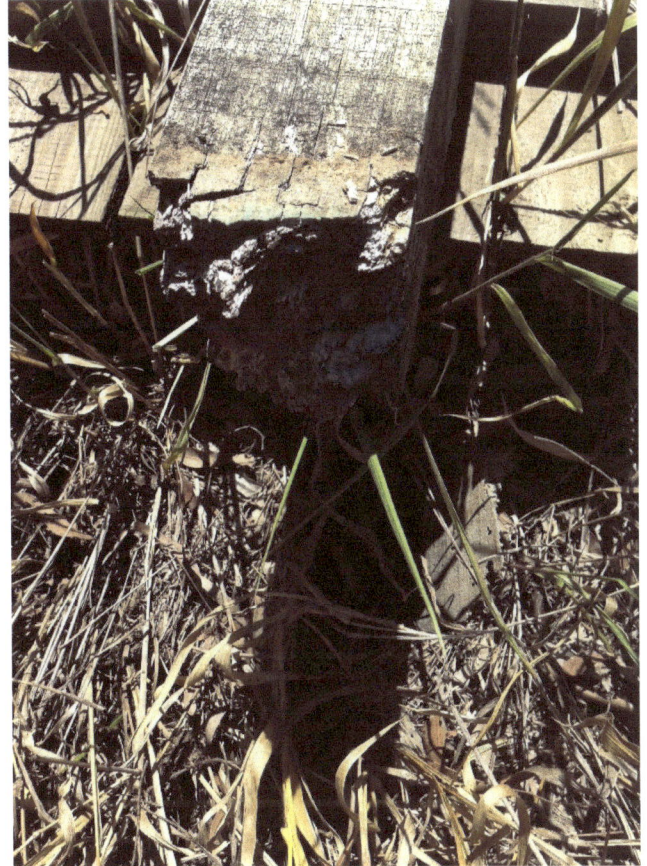

Fig. 16. This fence has failed as the hardwood posts were installed incorrectly.

Fig. 17. Decay of post in concrete at groundline.

Hardwood and cypress posts are prone to accelerated decay at the groundline if they are set in concrete. Cypress, the more so, if sapwood exceeds 20% of the cross section. Ensuring you receive Durability 1 In Ground hardwoods does not solve the problem. As the timber shrinks, a gap forms between the concrete and the post and moisture is held there by capillary action. This can promote decay. Also compounding the possibility of decay is the use of fertiliser and watering as is often found in a domestic setting.[17] Cypress and hardwood should not be set in concrete but, instead, use either no fines concrete, fine crushed rock or natural earth if suitable.

No fines concrete is made using aggregate with a 10 mm maximum size, 450kg cement per cubic metre of mix, and a water cement ratio of 0.55 and most importantly, no sand. The concrete must be

---

[17] One former colourful identity in the treatment industry used to refer to this as "Victa (as in the lawn mower) disease". It was more evident in settings where people nurtured their lawn with water and fertiliser.

manufactured to the requirements of AS 1379. To ensure a complete coating of the aggregate, it is particularly important that the concrete is well agitated immediately before placing. No fines concrete must be discharged directly into the holes within one hour of batching, and tamped without delay. Reworking destroys the bond with No-fines concrete. Ideally, the top 100 mm of a hole should be plugged with clay to prevent surface infiltration into the concrete though this is seldom possible. If the posts are to be load bearing, you should allow a suitable time, say four days, for the concrete to cure sufficiently.[18]

Where Durability Class 1 In Ground timber is not available, the life of posts such as jarrah can be extended by the use of a pole bandage. This product looks like a heavy duty bubble wrap except that the bubbles are filled with preservative, mainly boron and fluorine. When there is moisture in the timber, the prerequisite for decay, the preservative is drawn into the timber. This product can add up to another five or even more years to the life of in ground timber.[19] A pole bandage should not be used to counter the effect of installing a post in concrete.

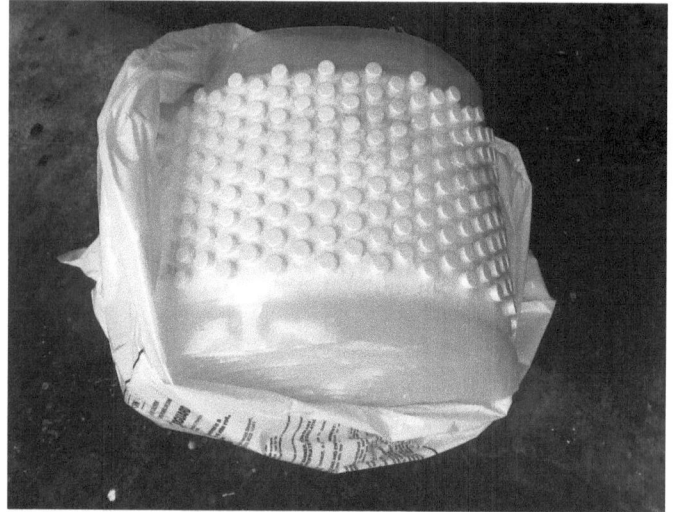

Fig. 18. Pole bandage.

I readily concede that cypress posts with low sapwood content have been used successfully in southern markets but it must also be conceded that it has been downgraded from In Ground 1 to In Ground 2 for a reason. In the cooler climates, it is probably adequate to just use no fines concrete but not in warmer climates where a bandage should also be introduced.

Shrinkwrap style bandages were developed by the CSIRO in the 1970's but Australian field trials proved that they created a microclimate under the bandage and hastened decay rather than delay it. These bandages are used and promoted in the UK where they are sold with a either a 20 or 40 year guarantee depending on the product. [20] Presumably, the climatic conditions make the difference.

---

[18] Timber Queensland. *Technical Data Sheet 9 Timber Retaining Walls*. (Brisbane: Timber Queensland. 2014) 5.

[19] One manufacturer of this type of product is Preschem (Australia) Pty. Ltd and is sold under the name *Bioguard Bandage*. This manufacturer claims its bandages are effective against white, brown and soft rot, an area where CCA has limited effectiveness.

[20] One such manufacturer is Postsaver Europe Ltd.

Fig. 19. Post depth needs special consideration in reactive soil.

The usual depth that a post supporting a fence that is up to 1.8m high is set in the ground is 600 mm. I have sold many fences with this embedment and, with the benefit of hindsight, I have to say that a good many of them started to fall over (including the fence in Figure Nineteen)! This is because half my town is built on the very fertile black Lockyer Valley soil that produces magnificent crops but is also highly reactive. Fences in the other areas give no trouble. This is where local knowledge is invaluable and it is seldom available when someone from a different area is quoting over the phone. If there is any suggestion of the soil being reactive, a 900 mm embedment should be specified.

The actual method of installing the post can vary. Figure Twenty shows the normal recommendation.[21] This arrangement has worked well but there are a few considerations. In my home area, ground line decay is in the top 450 mm and nothing much happens 600 mm deep and definitely nothing happened at 900 mm. But if you move further west where the top soil is drier, it can be more moist deeper down, the decay area likewise moves down and so the free draining gravel can then be important. A further consideration is that a gravel base does not suit a pre-cut post system. These have to have a base of concrete or no fines concrete set to a predetermined level . Again, local knowledge is important as is a preparedness to be flexible depending on the product being used. The most important consideration will be the ability to shed moisture sideways.

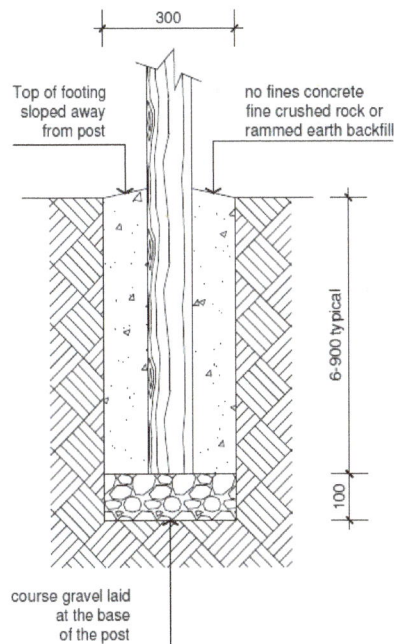

Fig. 20. Normal recommendation for installing hardwood posts.

Posts in Supports

---

[21] Timber Queensland. *Fences ...*, 2. Similarly Bailey, Ralph. *Pers. Com*. 18 November 2015.

The problems associated with putting timber in the ground can be avoided if the end of the post is kept above ground in a steel post support. But a set of well known problems can be swapped for ones that are different and less well understood.

Most "off the shelf" post supports are made for verandah posts which are braced back to the main house through the roof structure. The connection at the ground does not need to be very heavy and indeed invariably they are not. At best, they offer some stiffness in only one direction. I have seen fences mounted in supports that are very flimsy and almost "flap in the breeze". The support needs to offer

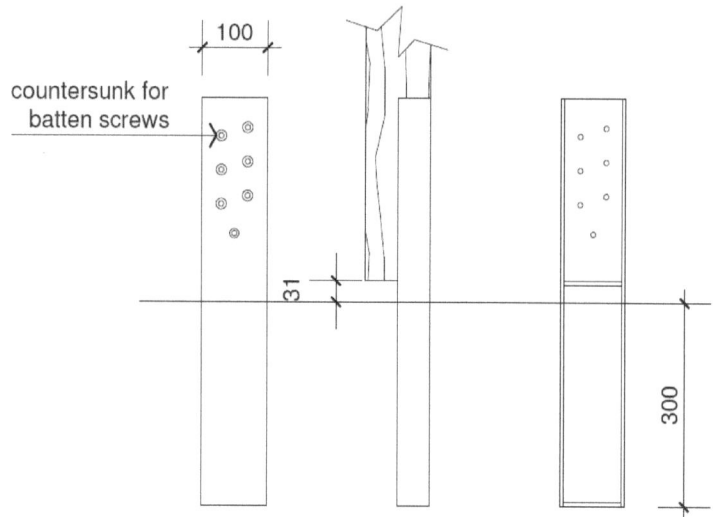

Fig. 21. Support made from C section steel.

resistance in all directions and we found that a very good way of doing this was with a custom support fabricated from C section steel.

Consideration should be given to additional corrosion resistance and this is dealt with in the chapter Steel Posts Used with Timber. There, the requirements for steelwork within 10 km of the coast is also addressed.

5. STEEL POSTS USED WITH TIMBER

It is not uncommon to see steel posts used in conjunction with timber rails and palings or other infill material. Presumably, this is thought to give a greater service life than timber which, in certain circumstances, it will. Conversely, in other circumstances it will provide a shorter service life. Like the use of timber, the use of steel has its own issues which must be attended to in the design, specification and supply stage.

Fig. 22. Corrosion at groundline.

Perhaps the most telling issue for steel posts is corrosion at groundline. The hot dipped galvanized post in Figure Twenty-two was only twelve years old when the image was taken and it is supporting a home, not a fence! While galvanizing can offer excellent corrosion resistance, surprisingly it can offer little resistance to pure rainwater.[22] Just as old galvanized iron tanks had to have a protective film[23] so, similarly, galvanized posts have to be protected at groundline. In the past, this could have been done very effectively by tar epoxy paints applied from a minimum of 100 mm below the groundline to just above it (say 50-100 mm). These proven paints have now been removed from the market due to concerns they may have been a carcinogen. Replacements are produced which also give good protection.[24]

Corrosion can also occur between the steel and any timber member, and hardwood in particular due to its acidity. My own practice would have been to apply a sacrificial epoxy paint coat[25] between the steel and the timber.

A further consideration is the thickness of the steel which, in turn, impacts the thickness of the galvanising. In an attempt to reduce costs the steel thickness can be reduced to as little as 3 mm or even less. The effect is to reduce a total galvanizing thickness from 500 grammes per m^2 (GSM) for 4 mm thick steel to approximately 390 grammes for 3 mm. The impact of this is to reduce the published life expectancy from 33-100 years in a C3 medium risk[26] application to 26 to 78 years.[27] My own practice

---

[22] The Lysaght Referee (27th edition) makes an important observation when it says, "High purity rain-water. . . is aggressive to galvanised steel tanks" which must reasonably apply also to galvanised posts. (Sydney: John Lysaght. 1985).192.

[23] This was done by inserting a bag of chemicals called a Tect-a tank prior to any rainwater entering the tank.

[24] One such replacement paint is PPG's Sigmashield 880/Amerlock 880, a two-component, high-build, polyamine adduct-cured epoxy coating and is mentioned as a standard which should be met or exceeded by the paint you specify/use.

[25] The product we used was white Knight Epoxy Enamel in an aerosol as it was the only one available in our locality. It is important that it is not the normal decorative style paint.

[26] Described as "Atmospheric environment with medium pollution … e.g. urban areas, coastal areas with with low deposition of chlorides". Galvanisers Association of Australia, *Atmospheric Corrosion Resistance of Hot Dipped Galvanized Coatings*. (Melbourne: Galvanisers Association of Australia. U.D) 6.

[27] Galvanisers Association of Australia. *Hot Dipped Galvanizing - The best protection inside and out*. (Melbourne: Galvanisers Association of Australia. U.D.) 6.

would not be to use anything less than 4 mm. The published life expectancies are based on atmospheric corrosion rates and may not match real life expectancy as groundline corrosion is likely to be the governing influence.

Should the application be in either of the higher risk C4 or C5[28] applications, galvanising would appear to be an imprudent choice based on the published life expectancy which is 17 to 33 years and 9 to 17 years respectively based on 4 mm steel. In these cases, stainless steel, (either 304 or 316 grade) should be used.[29] Alternatively, appropriate timber installed correctly will outlast galvanised steel.

Fig. 23. Spotted gum fence at Byron Bay

Fig. 24. Duragal style fence post

DuraGal style products, in my opinion, should not be used as fence posts as the coating thickness, which varies from 100 to 135 grammes per m[2],[30] is not sufficiently robust. This is much thinner than the already light coating you see on products such as triple grips) which is generally rated to the Z275 category (275 GSM total for both sides). Products made to the Z275 specification are regularly recommended not to be used at all for exterior applications.[31] The manufacturers of treated timber will only allow their timber against Z275 galvanising if the position is at least 8 km from the coast.[32]

[28] Coastal areas without spray and coastal areas respectively. Galvanisers Association of Australia, *Atmospheric Corrosion Resistance of Hot Dipped Galvanized Coatings.* (Melbourne: Galvanisers Association of Australia. U.D) 6.

[29] Pryda and other manufacturers require the stainless version of its steel products to be used within 10 km of the coast and Arch required stainless fitting to be used with timber treated with its waterborne chemicals when within eight km of the coast. See the full discussion in my book *Timber Preservation Guide.*

[30] OneSteel Trading. *DuraGal flooring System – Issue 6.* No publication information. 1.

[31] Compare the 135 GSM to say a Z or C purlins, used under a roof which are normally to Z350 (175 GSM per side) or even Z450 (225 GSM per side) specification.

[32] This is discussed in detail under corrosion in my Timber Preservation guide. Briefly, all timber is acidic to some degree, new preservatives are more corrosive and some steel manufacturers will not warrant their steel used in conjunction with

The steel post in Figure Twenty-four is a DuraGal type product installed directly in concrete without paint protection and is within metres of a swimming pool! As these can also be a hot dipped galvanised product, it is important to specify the galvanised coating thickness on your product to avoid such light levels of galvanising.

Image not available

Fig. 25. "Blooming" on powdercoated galvanised steel in C5 application.   **Fig. 26** Powdercoating flaking off steel.

Should a fully painted post be required, specifiers should avoid just saying "powdercoated" or indeed any other generic painting term but seek a written recommendation for preparation and finish from the paint manufacturer. Figure Twenty-five is on a bridge I supplied where the finish over the hot dipped galvanised rails was just mentioned as "powdercoated" and it subsequently bloomed. The environment it was being used in required a very costly, high performing, specialty product. You may consider including in your documentation that a certificate from the paint applicator be supplied stating that the coating meets the specification.

timber.

6. SIZES

The timber sizes in Table 1 reflect those that are normally used for domestic fences. These sizes seem to be driven more by tradition and experience than by science. The sizes are so expected that, if smaller, but structurally adequate posts were used, the fence would not look right. But obviously the hardwood posts are oversized if you are using structural timber. If an F5 pine in 90x90 mm will suffice, an F17[33] hardwood is well oversize at 100x100 mm.

Member	Hardwood	Cypress	Treated Pine
Corner and Gate Posts	100x100 mm	100x100 mm	90x90 mm
Intermediate Posts	100x75 mm	100x75 mm	90x70 mm
Rails	75x38 mm (2.1 m span)	75x50 mm (2.1 m span)	70x45 mm (2.1m span)
	100x38 mm (2.4 m span)	100x38 mm (2.4 m span)	90x35 mm (2.4 m span)
Table 1. Timber Sizes[34]			

My preference would be to substitute a 75x50 mm for a 100x38 mm for the rail as it has less spring if you are hand nailing your cladding.

With commercial fencing, sizes are going to be governed by the aesthetics you wish to achieve with only lip service given to structural requirements. It will be "lip service" as the sizes will generally be greater than the minimum required to meet the BCA and with which, after all, fencing does not have to comply. Using my calculations for F22 handrails[35] (and a high proportion of east coast hardwoods will be producing F22 in appearance grade unseasoned timber), to comply with the BCA handrail requirements the sizes and spans would need to be:

Posts for up to a 3.0 m span – 125x125 mm
Posts for up to 2.0 m span – 125x100 mm
Note: 150x150 posts in hardwood are not recommended.

Rails – 90x90 mm – 1.7 m single span, 2.3 m double span
170x69 mm aligned horizontally - 2.3 m single span, 3.0 m double span
170x44 mm aligned horizontally - 1.5 m single span, 2.0 m double span
145x69 mm aligned horizontally - 3.0 m single span, 2.0 m double span
145x44 mm aligned horizontally - 1.5 m single span, 2.0 m double span
145x44 mm aligned vertically - 1.5 m single span, 2.0 m double span
120x44 mm aligned vertically - 1.4 m single span, 1.9 m double span
 95x44 mm aligned vertically - 1.3 m single span, 1.7 m double span

The sizes I used most often were 200x100 for posts and 200x50 for rails. A post that has a section size of 100 mm thick will last a third longer than one that is only 75 mm thick so is preferred as installation costs will be the same.

---

[33] If the timber is of a respectable structural grade is almost certain to be F17 in most Queensland species. If it is of an acceptable appearance grade it will be F22.

[34] Timber. *Residential …*, 1.

[35] Refer to my *Commercial Barrier Guide*.

7. COMMERCIAL FENCING

Fig. 27. Spotted gum zoo fencing, Japan.

Fig. 28. Fence to subdivision, Brisbane.

The bright area for the fencing market is that of commercial fencing. This segment is where creativity from professional designers is realised through specification driven, low volume products, or at least that is the intention. Many of the Australian hardwoods are ideally suited for this application. The Japanese zoo fence in Figure Twenty-seven, manufactured to a much higher standard than the commercial fence in Figure Twenty-eight which itself is of a high standard,[36] illustrates the level that these fences can achieve. Commercial fencing should take our thinking to a whole new level, far above that of domestic fencing.

Fig. 29 Landscaping sleepers used for commercial fencing, Gold Coast.

Someone attempted to copy[37] the look of the subdivision fence (Figure Twenty-eight) at an entry statement on the Gold Coast (Figure Twenty-nine). Whereas the Brisbane fence was a success, the entry statement shows that intention and reality sometimes do not match. A successful commercial fence starts with a suitable specification,

---

[36] Supplied by me c. 2000 and still in good order in 2015.

[37] I say "copy" as when I was out driving with a friend he saw the fence from a distance and said it was mine and that we should stop and photograph it for the records.

which may well have been the case here. Having been in this particular market for many years, I have seen case after case of where specifications were ignored but, without the specification, any argument with the supplier/installer is pointless. In this case, what has happened is that the sizes specified for the statement are sizes that can also be supplied as low grade landscaping sleepers. That is not a problem in itself as I did the same. But there is a big difference between a specification for a landscaping sleeper which says "one reasonable edge and one reasonable face" and structural hardwood let alone one step further to appearance grade durable hardwood. Careful purchasing and a good relationship with your supplier is necessary. As a landscaping sleeper may well be a third the price of appropriate timber there is always a danger that it is substituted in an attempt to either win the contract or to maximise profits.

For timber suitable for commercial fencing, it is necessary to specify beyond the requirements of the different timber standards as they generally only relate to strength at the time of milling. The designer must be concerned with appearance and longevity. Suitable specifications would be:

Pine
Posts, MGP12 or F8, Incised to 10mm, treated to H4. Incising done after dressing
Rails, MGP12 or F8, Incised to 10mm, treated to H4[38]. Incising done after dressing

Cypress
Posts, F7 cut with heart in centre, maximum 20% sapwood
Rails, F7, maximum 20% sapwood

Hardwood
Posts, Structural Grade 2, free of heart for sizes under 175x175, in the following species.
       East coast: Spotted gum, tallowwood, ironbark, grey gum, Gympie M\messmate
       West coast: jarrah in association with pole bandage
Standard rails (Figure Twenty-eight), Sapwood treated to H3 and not to exceed 20% of cross section
       East coast: Spotted gum, tallowwood, ironbark, grey gum, Gympie M\messmate
       West coast: jarrah in association with pole bandage

Quality Rails (Figure Twenty-seven), Structural Grade 1, free of heart, in the following species.
       East coast: Spotted gum, tallowwood, ironbark, grey gum, Gympie M\messmate
       West coast: Jarrah
       Sapwood treated to H3

Note: Hardwood has the additional consideration of colour. Figures Twenty-seven and Twenty-eight show quality handrail and standard rails both in spotted gum but prepared in two different ways. The first is treated then dressed for maximum visual effect and the other is rough sawn and treated giving maximum durability. A third way of preparing hardwood is to dress the timber and then treat it. This has the advantage of covering the different colours that a mix of species will have. You must expect this if you have only specified to a F grade and not nominated a single species. For normal use this is my preferred process as there are no treated shavings to deal with.

Note: for the smaller sizes in domestic fencing I have recommended using Durability Class 1 In Ground timber but here I am permitting a spotted gum, a Durability 2 In Ground timber. The differences are, higher quality, larger section size and the relatively short life cycle of public landscaping and of course, years of experience.

Modern processing with planers and CNC routing means that you can have virtually anything you can design. The planer may require custom tooling which initially is expensive but amortised over a number of items can still

---

[38] Granted that the rails are only a H3 application but the practicalities of processing the order are that machine setup time must be minimised. To change the incisor from say a 200x100 post to a 200x50 rail is only one quick step. To then change each head to incise only 8mm instead of 10 is an additional four changes.

be affordable. The CNC is infinitely variable and just needs a program written. When I first started to manufacture commercial fencing I had to use drill presses and chisel and chain morticers but a CNC machine can make the holes more accurately and quicker and does not demand a square cornered hole.

Tip: My experience has been that when working with CNC processed timber it is best to have the associated steelwork laser cut as well. Prepare the steelwork first and check the first CNC worked component with the steel. Recalibrate as needed. Small differences in handmade steel are not compatible with the precision of CNC produced items. One project I recall changed the fabrication time with hand fabricated steel components from 12 -15 minutes to 3 minutes for laser cut,.

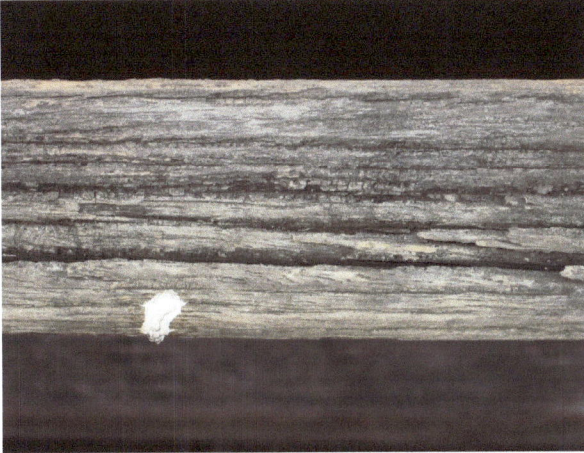

Fig. 30. Degrade of flat handrail top after approx. 20 years.

Fig. 31. Similar size rail detailed to shed moisture.

When designing commercial landscaping it is important to detail all members so they shed moisture. The top of posts should not be flat, but sloping or capped. Capping is critical for heart in posts typically 150x150[39] and up. Even the top of rails that are only 50 mm will degrade and a little care and tooling minimises this. Designers are very willing to utilise the strength of timber, that is its natural beauty, and rightly so, but the corollary is that its weaknesses should likewise be accommodated.

Fig. 32. The diagonal configuration of a top rail has proved very effective.

---

[39] Refer to my *Seven Deadly Sins of External Timber Design* where I advise against using this size.

Fig. 33. protruding bolts are dangerous.

The need for enhanced aesthetics and public safety requires that more thought be given to the fasteners than would be the case with domestic fencing. Care has to be taken to avoid protruding bolts which can cause injuries. The nut should as a minimum be countersunk with no protruding thread. This tends to be unsightly and my preference would be to use a sleeve nut. A tamper resistant head reduces the incidence of vandalism as well as more than a shifting spanner is needed to remove them. Within 8-10 kilometres of the coast, stainless should be used to comply with different manufacturers' recommendations.

Tip: When using sleeve nuts, assemble with a Loctite style product on the bolt thread.

Fig. 34. Custom post made by the author.

Fig. 35 Lower price substitute used in next stage.

A designer should consider how differently the same design can be interpreted by different manufacturers. Figures Thirty-four and Thirty-five illustrate this. The differences are:

- sleeve nuts verses countersunk nuts
- timber processed then treated verses treated then processed

- Tanalith E/ACQ verses CCA
- grooved, assembled and then the tops cut verses all theoretical measurements
- one set in no fines concrete (not visible from image) and the other not, and
- dimensions sanded off verses dimensions left on timber

The designer should provide more than basic dimensions but provide fabrication details as needed to achieve the finish envisaged. A well detailed commercial fence does not happen by accident with the lowest price tenderer!

8. SPECIALISED FENCING

Noise Barriers

The effectiveness of a noise barrier is dependent on its height. Generally speaking, the top of a noise barrier dissects the line between a point 1m above the noise source (on a road surface that is both carriageways) and a point 1.5m above the floor of the affected residence/s. This includes the second story of a multi story building. In practical terms that means that the wall can be very high and the RTA generally stop at 8m high as anything higher is visually unacceptable.[40] Clearly, such fences are outside the scope of this book. But in a normal suburban setting on level ground, traffic noise can be reduced by as much as 10 decibels[41] so long as there are no gaps in the fence and the material weighs 10 kg per m2, which can be met with 20 mm pine[42] (so avoid the normal 16 mm residential paling and best to go to 25 mm) and 16 mm hardwood. Because of the lower grades of timber generally used, particular attention has to be given to the potential consequences of warping and shrinkage over time.

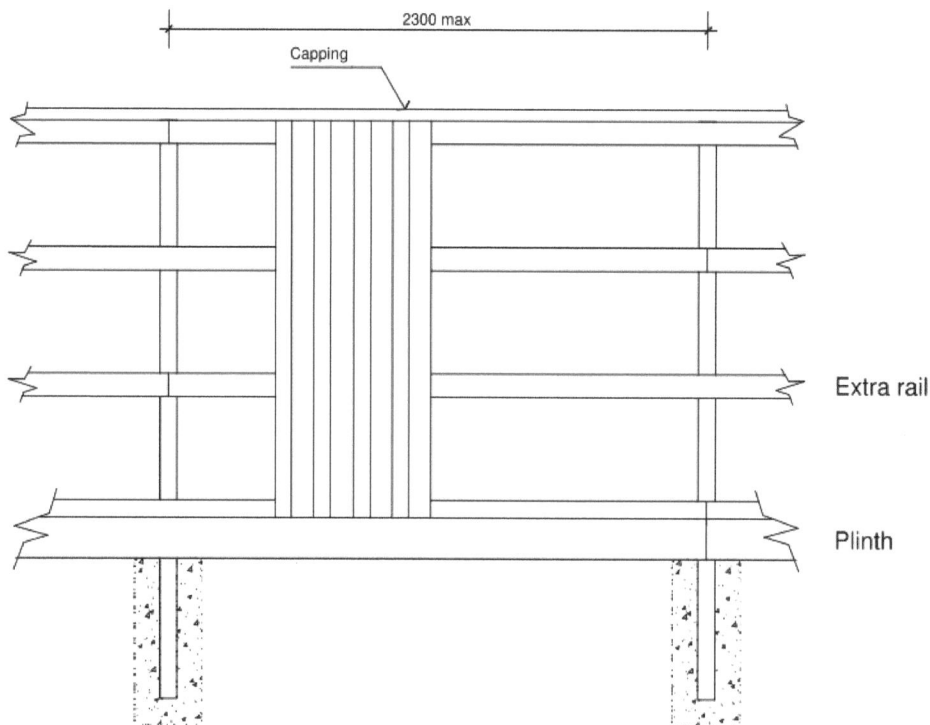

Fig. 36. Sound fence layout.

While a sound fence is generally along the same lines as a standard 1.8 m high residential fence there are differences. The Vicroads guidelines differ from those in Timber Queensland's Technical Data Sheet, *Residential Timber Fences* in that the Queensland guidelines require an extra rail and Victoria requires a greater overlap of palings (35 mm compared to 25 mm) and a maximum bay width of 2.3 m.[43] given there is a target figure of noise reduction from the Victorian design, it would be prudent to

---

[40] Roads and Traffic Authority. *Noise Wall Design Guidelines*. (RTA: 2007), 3.

[41] An increase of 10 decibels roughly corresponds to a doubling of the perceived loudness. RTA. *Noise* …, 9.

[42] Vicroads. *A Guide to the Reduction of Traffic Noise,* (Vicroads. 1994, reprinted 2003), 8.

[43] Timber. *Residential* …, 4 and Vicroads. *Guide* …, 9-10.

combine the best features of both as seen in Figure Thirty-six.

Further differences from a residential fence is an obligatory cap to stop movement in the end of the palings and a plinth to ground level to fill any gap under the fence. The plinth should be of the same durable material as the posts.

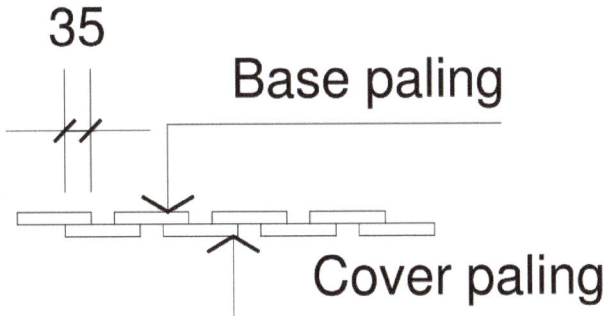

Fig. 37. Cover paling detail.

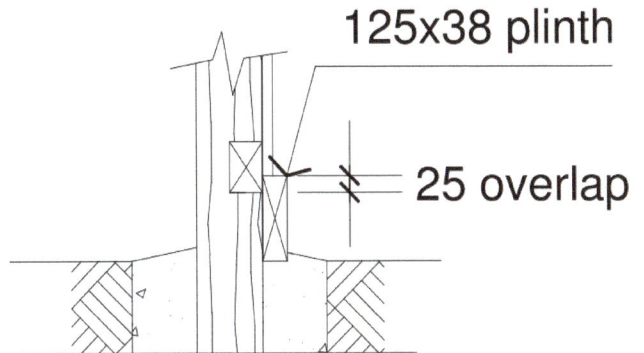

Fig. 38. Plinth detail.

The New Zealand experience is that H5 treated pine can provide a 50 year design life and that people often preferred timber to other types of sound barrier. They are also fast to build from simple readily available plans. Of course there is the added benefit of less embodied carbon than concrete and steel. On the negative side, they also observed that often what was installed was a boundary fence, not an acoustic fence and that inadequate timber quality, poor design and poor construction practices meant that a shorter life was actually achieved.[44] The RTA by comparison recommend timber only be for sound barriers used in exceptional circumstances due to poor experiences with CCA treated sleepers.[45] If they were CCA treated, they were landscaping sleepers and were never fit to build anything which requires a long service life. They also mention issues with fire. Afterglow is a well known problem with CCA and for large walls the new replacement chemicals, Tanalith E or ACQ, should be used.

Pool Fencing

Pool fencing is highly regulated by various government and local authority regulations. While there is a swimming pool safety standard (AS 1926.1 and 2) this can be modified by the regulating authority. This means that before starting on a pool fence you should make yourself aware of the latest requirements for your area. The ease that children can still climb this fencing, as shown in Figure Thirty-nine, illustrates that even a correctly installed pool fence will not negate the need for diligence by the pool owners.

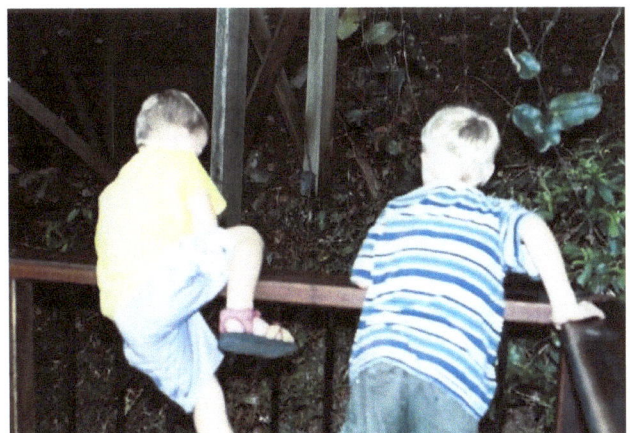

Timber is very suitable for pool fences as it does not rust. The basics for a pool fence in Queensland are:

Fig. 39. Pool fencing is not childproof

---

[44] New Zealand Transport Agency. *State Highway Noise Barrier Design Guide, Version 1.0.* (Self published. 2010), 59.

[45] RTA. *Noise …*, 52.

- top of fence is 1200 mm
- no gap more than 100 mm under the fence or gate
- the maximum spacing of the verticals is 100 mm when the rails are on the inside
- If the spacing is more than 10 mm the rails shall be 900 mm minimum apart.
- the distance from the fence top to the top of the bottom trail exceeds 1100 mm

When the rails are on the outside, a combination that assists climbing, there appears to be no minimum distance between the rails if the gap is less than 10 mm but it is prudent to maintain the 900 mm gap required for spaced palings.

Note: The problem with the figures mentioned above is that they do not allow for shrinkage. The test for a complying gap under AS1926 1-2—7 requires that a cone with a large end diameter of 105 mm will not pass when a force of 150 newtons is exerted at the midpoint. A 100 mm unseasoned paling, spaced at 100 mm will have a theoretical gap of 106 mm after seasoning. The gap should not exceed 95 mm at the time of laying. If aiming for a maximum of 10 mm gap use a laying gap of 3.0mm.

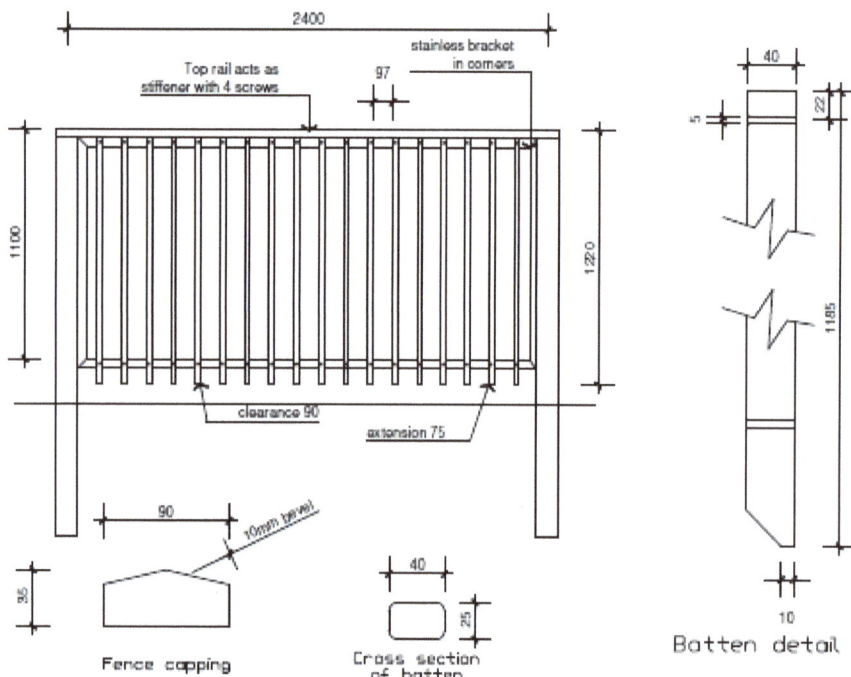

MANUFACTURING INSTRUCTIONS

MATERIAL

90x90 dressed Dur 1 IG post
45x45 dressed Dur 1 AG rail (2/2.4, 2.12)
40x25 dressed Dur 1 AG slat (18/1.2)
90x35 dressed Dur 1 AG rail (1/4.8)
75x14 stainless batten screw (8 only)
65x10 stainless steel screw (36 only)
75x75x75 stainless angles (4 only)
25x10 stainless pan hd screw (16 only)

Fig. 40. Concept modular swimming pool fence.

This type of fence ideally suits a prefabricated module, just as the steel and aluminium pool fence manufacturers do. Figure Forty shows a concept of what is possible in a full timber fence. Infills could also be stainless steel bars.

9. PLYWOOD FENCING

Though not very common in domestic fences, plywood can be used in considerable quantities in commercial fencing such as around subdivisions. Plywood has proven to be very effective and provide a reasonable life when installed correctly. For success the plywood must:

- use an A Bond[46] glue
- be preservative treated to H3 (LOSP is not recommended)
- not touch the ground
- be double sided with a capping rail, and
- be finished with a waterproof paint/sealant

Sizes

The normal size plywood that is stocked is 2400x1200 mm with 2700 mm high sometimes being available. Generally fences will be 1.8 m high and while this is not normally available as a stocked item as either 1.8 m or 0.9 m it can be produced to order. Before specifying something that is not available off the shelf confirm its availability[47]. Thicknesses produced are 4.5, 7, 9, 12, 15, 17, 19, 21 and 25.

Fig. 41. Ply fence panels inbetween a timber fence.

Structural grades

There are three types of plywood that would perform adequately, Marine, Structural and Exterior. Plywood can also be graded from F8 to F34 dependant on the quality of the veneers and the timber species used. An F grade would be applicable to Marine and Structural ply but Australian exterior plywood manufactured to AS/NZS 2271 is not structurally graded. Due to cost, Exterior plywood is most likely to be specified. The lack of an F grade is of no concern as the design of the fence is not going to be governed by structural considerations in the same way a plywood floor joist will be. The design considerations will be that it is thick enough and supported closely enough so as not to warp and that it not be easy to vandalise.

Face Grades

Structural plywood is manufactured with a variety of face grades being:

- A - highly quality appearance grade and suitable for all finishes
- S - an appearance grade that permits, on agreement between specifier and manufacturer, natural characteristics such as knots, holes and discolouration to be promoted as a decorative feature.
- B - an appearance grade suitable for high quality (but not gloss) paint finishing

---

[46] Produced from a phenol formaldehyde (PF) resin and forms a permanent glueline that will not deteriorate under wet conditions, heat or cold e.g. used in the manufacture of Marine and Structural plywoods.

[47] A list of manufacturers can be supplied by the PAA.

- C - non appearance grade with a solid surface in that all permissible open defects have been filled and sanded (one of the most common grades), and
- D - as for C except that the faces allow open defects such as splits and holes. (one of the most common grades),

Most plywood applications only have one exposed face so, for economy, it can be ordered with a mixed grade, say AD grade. But just as exterior plywood does not come in structural grades, the standard face specifications above do not apply. It is described as having "one high grade face and a reduced grade on the back."[48] An A grade face only needs to be specified if a clear finish (not a good idea for fencing) or a high gloss paint finish will be used.

Finishing

The PAA maintain they have carried out exhaustive tests and recommend that, for best results, only high quality 100% acrylic paint systems should be used externally.[49] (It warns also that this paint is not compatible with treatments that contain wax.). Elsewhere in their publications they say that as well as the paint, you can use a high quality water repellent stain. Further, it is critical that **only** light reflective colours such as white be used and never dark colours such as mission brown or black. The edges should be sealed using the same paint finish used on the face because moisture is more readily absorbed through the end grain.. This is easiest done when still in the pack. The plywood sheets should be pre-primed before installing, at least on the frame side, as it will not be possible to apply paint where it is needed after installing the sheets. Paint will not be sufficient protection. The ply must be rot proofed to H3 by chemical treatment.[50] In addition, in humid areas where there is a possibility of mould growth, it is recommended that a quality mouldicide be added to the paint.[51]

Plywood can be purchased with a machined/textured face veneer. This is highly recommended as it is a better surface to hold paint and also "reduces and disguises any surface checking of the face veneer effectively by dispersing or reflecting the incidence of solar radiation."[52]

Branding

The plywood should specified as being PAA certified. Designers need to be aware of the dangers of contractors substituting imported plywood as international standards can differ from those in Australia.[53] The plywood supplied should be branded with:

- the manufacturer's name
- the word "Exterior"
- the face grade, back grade and bond (e.g. AC-A Bond)
- the Standard No. i.e. AS/NZS 2271
- the formaldehyde emission class (e.g. E0)[54]

---

[48] PAA. *Product and Specification Guide for the Professional and Home Handyperson*. (PAA, no publication details) 10.

[49] PAA. *Facts About Plywood – 2012 Edition*. (PAA. No publication details) 23.

[50] Specify the more robust treatments such as CCA or ACQ. There have been issues with LOSP in more difficult environments.

[51] PAA. *Featuring Plywood in Buildings, Revision 5*. (PAA. No publication Details) 16.

[52] PAA. *Featuring ...*, 11-12.

[53] The differences in the amount of chemical used for the equivalent of our H3 treatment is outlined in my *Timber Preservation Guide*.

[54] PAA. *Product ...*, 9.

In the event of a substitution product, when large quantities are involved, as they can be with residential subdivisions, it would be prudent to have product checked for compliance with Australian Standards.[55]

Installation

Fig. 42. Deteriorating plywood fence.

The plywood fence shown in Figure 42 is constructed using CCH's Shadowclad but it is important to note that it does not follow any of the ply manufacturers recommendations for a successful outcome.

Plywood with a textured surface which is made for walling will have a smooth face which would otherwise be protected from the weather. When used as fencing, this face would then be exposed to the weather and be outside of the manufacturers guidelines. Unless you have written advice to the contrary, the fence should be clad on both sides and follow carefully the manufactured instructions for domestic wall construction. The fence should also have a cap on the top that protects the top edges from the weather.

Fasteners

When treated timber is used externally within 8 km of the coast, a minimum of 304 stainless fasteners (or monel[56] in nails) are required.[57] In all other circumstances galvanised can be used. Recommended fasteners are as follows:[58]

- If a hand driven nail is used, it should be a minimum of a 40x2.8 mm flat head driven flush with the surface.
- Where a machine driven nail is used it should be a minimum of a 50x2.8 mm flat head again driven flush with the surface.
- In both instances a stainless nail may not provide enough grip in this application as the shank provides little grip compared to HDG.
- Where the ply is screwed, use a minimum of a Type 17 without a countersunk head and the size should be 10x50 for hardwood[59]

---

[55] Refer to PAA for a suitable laboratory in your State.

[56] Monel is the name given to a group of nickel alloys, primarily composed of nickel (up to 67%) and copper, with small amounts of iron, manganese, carbon, and silicon. It is very corrosion resistant in a marine environment.

[57] Corrosion in treated timber along with manufacturers' recommendations is discussed in my *Timber Preservation Guide*.

[58] These fastener recommendations are drawn from CHH. *Shadowclad Installation Guide, March 2014.* (CHH. No publication details) 1.

[59] CHH do not give a recommended screw for pine or hardwood framing. The 10x50 countersunk screw is a common size for domestic decking and should not be used. Our experience is that an 8# screw can snap when used with hardwood

Fastening Details

The edges of the sheets should ideally be fully supported but where an overhang cannot be avoided the fastener should not be more than 100 mm from the edge of the sheet. The fasteners should be no more than 150 mm apart in the top and bottom and vertical edges and the intermediate supports can be at 300 mm. The fasteners should also be no closer than 9 mm from the edge. When a shiplap profile is used, the fastener needs to be kept away from the lap and the weather groove.[60] Start fixing from one corner ensuring the sheet is square. If laps are used, or shiplaps, they should be aligned so as to be against the prevailing winds. The additional requirements for grooved sheets are that you do not fix them horizontally and you do not nail in the groove.

It is necessary to allow a gap of 3 to 5 mm between the vertical joints and corners to allow for expansion. This means that vertical supports every 2.4 m centres will not work with 2.4 m sheets though there are proprietary products designed to suit this spacing.[61] Care needs to be taken to ensure this is not overlooked by the builder as the temptation will be to plane off the edge sealed with paint.

It is necessary to keep the bottom of the plywood at least 100 mm above paving[62] or 150 mm above soil.[63] I recommend that you prepare very detailed drawings of the installation and have them approved by the specified supplier before issuing the plans. There are differences between the generic information given by PAA and CHH and this may be the case with other suppliers. Discussions prior to starting your drawings are very important.

---

framing. An 8# screw you would expect would suffice for pine as it is heavier than the recommended nail and has much better holding capacity. Confirm the screw size for pine with the ply manufacturer.

[60] These fixing recommendations are drawn from CHH. *Shadowclad ...*, 1-2.

[61] One such product is CHH's *Shadowclad.*

[62] CHH. *Shadowclad ...*, 1 (Figure 4).

[63] PAA. *Featuring ...*, 13.

10. HARDWARE

When it comes to hardware specifically designed for fencing there is a distinct, but not total dearth on the Australian market. The UK market by comparison has an embarrassment of riches with ready availability to specialised hardware including:

- bolt down post supports made from galvanised or painted steel.
- drive in post supports made from galvanised or painted steel.
- assorted galvanised fence panel fixing brackets
- assorted galvanised fence rail brackets
- assorted fence panel brackets from reconstituted timber and resin.

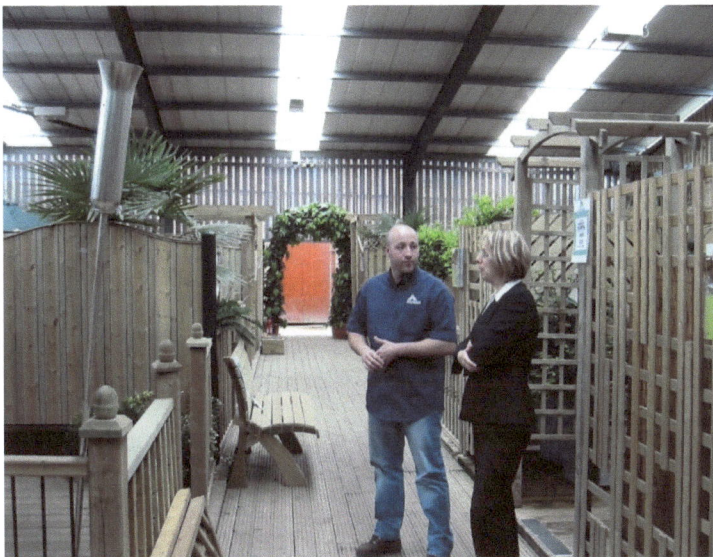

Fig. 43. A UK miller retailing premade fence panels.

The availability of this hardware in conjunction with readymade fencing panels means that UK purchasers have access to fences that can be erected relatively inexpensively[64] and quickly by inexperienced workers. While these prefabricated fences are flimsy by Australian standards,[65] their low cost means that they can be replaced or updated to one of the myriad of optional styles just as easily. The different climatic conditions in the UK impact greatly on what the minimum needs to be as indeed they do in Australia's wide climactic range.

Earlier in this guide I have made reference to different items of hardware such as custom fabricated post supports and tube nuts for safety in commercial landscaping. The emphasis of this chapter is on more readily available items. I have also briefly made mention of where to use galvanised or stainless fasteners which needs to be expanded upon. The specification of screws is clear cut. Screw durability is specified under AS 3566 Screws - Self-drilling - For the building and construction industries, which was introduced in 1988 in an attempt to counter the poor performance of imported fasteners particularly. Previously, compliance was to a material specification where products were deemed to comply if they had a certain coating thickness. The new standard adopted a stringent performance specification based on real life testing. For example, the test site for coastal use has to be "located less than 500 m from the

[64] A simple overlap fence panel, 1.8x1.8m can be purchased retail for under $39.00 (exchange rate $1au = £0.49)   A 30 metre run with good ground conditions can be installed in approximately 11 to 12 hours including logistics. Keighton. *Pers.Com.* 7 January 2016.

[65] Typically these are made from 100x6 mm pine and can be cut with the wane on the edge. They are stiffened by five and sometimes six vertical battens typically 25x18 mm frequently attached with heavy staples. The posts are only 75x75. Keighton. *Pers.Com.* 7 January 2016. These dimensions mean that the panels have about one third of volume of a minimalist pine fence.

mean high water line, in a coastal area with surf for most of the year".[66] The Standard has four classes of corrosion resistance:

Class 1	For general internal use where corrosion resistance is of minor importance. Most ZINC/YELLOW drywall and chipboard screws are in this category.
Class 2	For general internal use where significant levels of condensation occur. Electroplated ZINC/YELLOW is generally used to meet this class.
Class 3	For general external use in mild industrial and marine applications. The class is intended for roofing and cladding screws in mild applications.
Class 4	For external use in marine and moderately severe corrosive environments, generally within 1 kilometre from marine surf, although topography and /or strong prevailing winds may extend this distance.
Table 2. Different classes of screws.[67]	

Should you decide you are aiming for 50 a year life (and a correctly installed ironbark post can reach that), there seems little choice in the fasteners. They must be stainless (grade 304 or 316) as it is a simple matter of install and forget. Issues of corrosion in zinc screws are well enough known to discount them immediately irrespective of the class they are given. But why not galvanized or any Class 4 screw? One reputable manufacturer does say that their screws are suitable for 50 years in a light industrial/urban application which most fencing installations will be.[68] There are two reasons for not using them:

- The need for maintenance. The manufacturer who gives the 50 year industrial/urban life has a requirement "that areas not exposed to rain should be washed down regularly. . . . Washing should be carried out at least every six months and more frequently in coastal areas and areas of heavy industrial fallout"[69]
- Whatever you specify has the danger of being substituted with a lower priced and thence the likelihood of a lower performing product.

There is very minimal corrosion with large areas of galvanised (as you would have in a frame) and stainless screws so issues of dissimilar metals are of no concern. Corrosion only becomes an issue when there is a large section of stainless and a galvanised screw.[70] There can be a problem when using class four self drilling screws to attach the rail through a non-drilled galvanised post as the less well corrosion protected shaft and black steel of the frame, and the swarf created through drilling, are in contact.

Bolts and nails are a far more complex matter as there is a wide range of recommendations of where to use galvanised and where to use stainless or monel. Bolts, unlike screws, are not a performance based product. In my book, *Deck and Boardwalk Design Essentials,* I write about and illustrate the deteriorating performance of imported galvanised bolts. For this reason alone I would urge designers to specify stainless bolts. In my *Timber Preservation Guide* there is a detailed examination of recommendations and real life testing so I present only a summary here.

- all hardwoods are acidic, some to the point of corroding bolts

[66] http://www.buildex.com.au/corrosion_management.html. Date accessed. June 7, 2015.
[67] http://www.buildex.com.au/corrosion_management.html. Date accessed. June 7, 2015.
[68] http://www.buildex.com.au/climaseal4.html. Date accessed. June 7, 2015.
[69] http://www.buildex.com.au/buildex_warranty.html. Date accessed. June 7, 2015.
[70] Collinson, Dave. Technical Manager, Buildex ITW. *Pers. Com.* April 2015.

- new timber preservatives are up to three times more corrosive than CCA
- real life corrosion studies in New Zealand have shown that corrosion of the bolt shaft can be even more severe away for a direct marine environment.
- real life corrosion studies back up Arch Chemicals recommendations that stainless be used within 8 km of **any** coast (protected or surf) and Pryda's recommendation that all external brackets be stainless.[71]

As far as the actual fasteners to be used, the normal domestic fence rail to the post normally only requires a single 10 mm bolt or a single type 17, 14 gauge batten screw. Because of the corrosion issues, my preference would be for a 304 grade stainless batten screw, but use two if the posts are not checked to provide a seat for the rail. The screw length should be 75 mm for a 38 mm thick rail and 100 mm for a 50 mm rail. Some guides allow nailing but with much better fixings being readily available I would not recommend them.

For hand driven nails on hardwood palings use bullet head nails and with pine the nails must be flat or dome head. As for length, one industry recommendation is that, "Nails for 15 mm thick palings shall be either 50 x 2.8 mm (hand driven) or 45 x 2.5 mm (gun nails). Note: Longer nails are required for thicker palings and for lapped sound fences" and that "Nails into treated pine shall have deformed shanks."[72] Another says, "Nail lengths should be sized to allow a minimum penetration of 25 mm into hardwood and 35 mm into softwood … [and] twist shank are preferred for softwood."[73] When looking at the performance of the 45x2.5 mm gun nails in pine, I would personally use the same size nail as a hand driven nail (refer to case history *Residential Subdivision, Laidley*).

Testing the hold down ability of 18 different decking nails by the Forest and Wood Products Association led to the conclusion that "nails ain't nails"[74] This has led Timber Queensland to issue the following warning when specifying nails - *"large recent comparative laboratory withdrawal tests carried out by Timber Queensland on a wide range of commercially available machine driven nails indicated a large variation in machine nail withdrawal resistance. Installers of decking should ensure that machine nails used have equal or better withdrawal resistance than the hand nails given above. Installers should obtain comparative withdrawal information from nail suppliers or conduct comparative trials (pinch bar) on test material before using a particular machine nail".[75]* The hold down value of two 50x2.8 mm galvanised hand nails into a hardwood joist was found to be 2.6 kN but one gun nail tested as low as 1 kN and several tested under 2 kN while 8 gauge stainless screws tested at almost 11 kn! I suggest that 2.8 kN be the target as the hold down value for the two nails, even on fences.

At the time of writing, the major manufacturers of metal nailplates and brackets, with nationwide coverage, had very little in the line of fencing brackets. I was able to find one smaller manufacturer, Maclock Products in Brisbane that was relatively comprehensive in what they offered but unfortunately these brackets only had a limited retail presence.

---

[71] There is uniformity among nailplate manufacturers over the use of stainless externally but not from treatment chemical manufacturers.

[72] Timber. *Residential ...,* 2.

[73] Timber Advisory Service. Timber Fences. (Surry Hills: Self published, 2003), 15. This recommendation was before testing referred to later in this paragraph.

[74] Hayward, David and Colin Mackenzie. *Deck Nail Withdrawal Tests*. Forest and Wood Products Association Project 02.1209. No Publication details, 9.

[75] Timber Queensland. *Technical Datasheet 4, Residential Timber Decks*. (Brisbane: Self Published, 2014), 5.

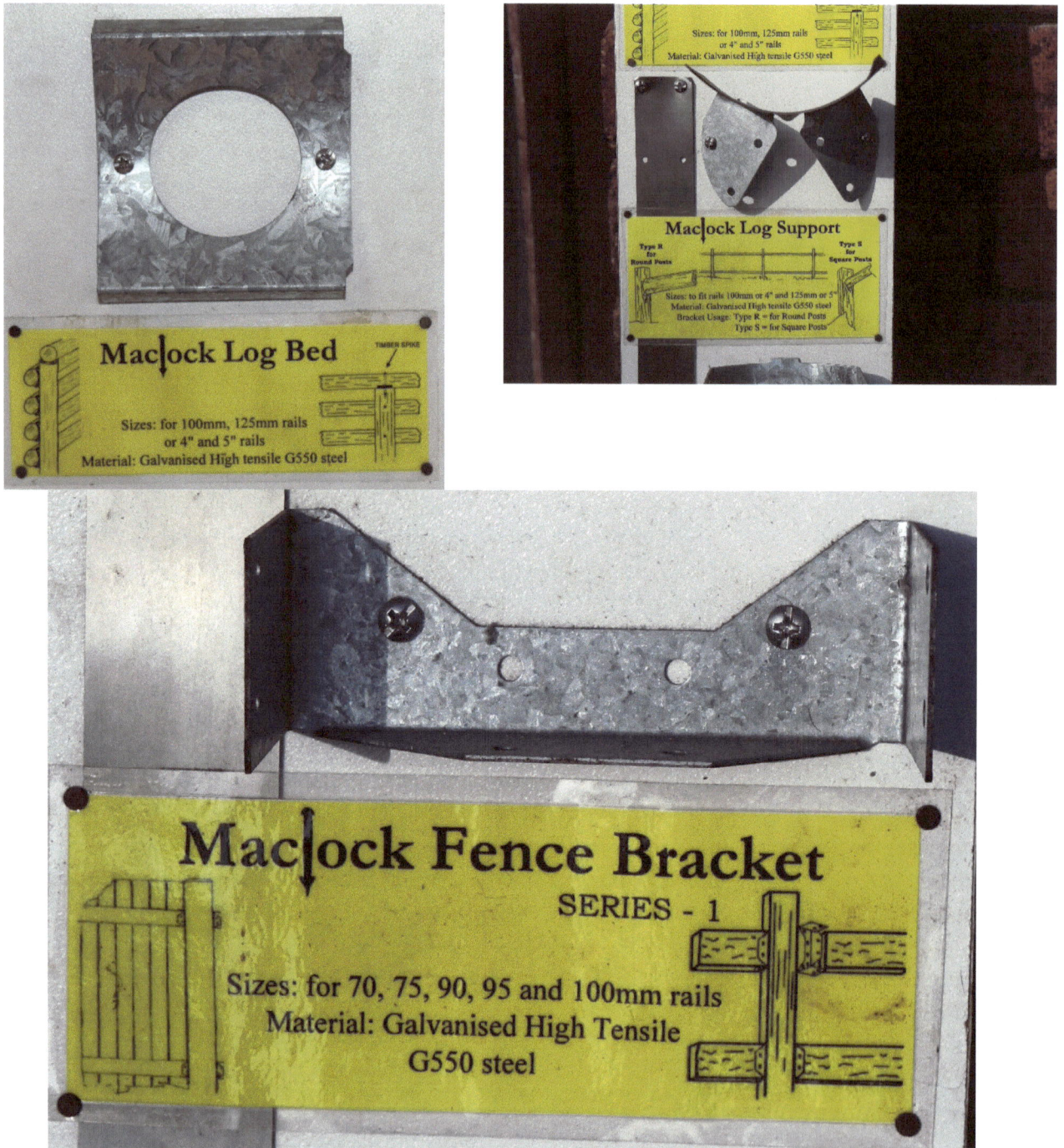

Fig. 44. Proprietary Fencing brackets

Lonza, a major supplier of treatment chemicals, requires stainless hardware be used in conjunction with treated timber within 8 km of the coast and Pryda requires stainless in all external applications.[76] Likewise these fencing brackets should also be stainless and fortunately this is an option. Where stainless is not an option they should be, at a very minimum, painted with a tar epoxy style paint similar to the galvanised post supports.

---

[76] Refer to my *Timber Preservation Guide* for a detailed discussion of corrosion in conjunction with treated timber.

11. FINISHING

Timber fences frequently have no finishing coats applied and are left to weather to a silver grey which is a reasonable decision when suitable materials have been used. But weather exposure does lead to premature degradation of the timber surfaces, whether it is through UV effects or water absorption. Checking, cracking, delaminating, discoloration, twisting and bowing can all be minimised by caring for your fence. Timber coatings do not necessarily improve the timber's resistance to decay and can, in fact, increase the risk substantially as they can reduce the ability of the timber to dry out. On the other hand, they minimise weathering and the potential for fungal organisms to develop on the surface if there is any moisture. Only choose to paint your fence if there is a commitment to maintain that paint in good order. The finishing of plywood is covered in that chapter.

Paint

Paint is a very reasonable choice of finishes especially now that we can see manufacturers warranting their product for unheard of lengths of time. One manufacturer warrants the paint for as long as you live in the house while another mentions 100 seasons. What is causing the change in paint? As one paint chemist said, "They are finally pulling their head out of the sand regarding the variability of timber".[77] Considering the difficulties with timber, the following all impact on the success:

Fig. 45. Painted fence.

- high to low amounts of extractives,
- high to low pH,
- high to low shrinkage on unseasoned timber (13 to 3 %)
- continual dimension change with moisture content change,
- surface finishes from rough to smooth,
- high to low densities,
- backsawn or quartersawn,
- great variability in absorption and
- great variability in grain characteristics.

The wonder is that paint succeeds at all with the stresses this variability can impose!

Generally, you cannot go wrong if you follow the manufacturer's recommendations but I am not so sure that is always the case with paint. Recommendations can vary between paint manufacturers which can again be different to timber industry recommendations which frequently require primers. In Table 3, I give in summary form the recommendations of four different paint manufacturers for primers on external acrylic paint.

---

[77] My source would rather not be named.

Dulux Weathershield Gloss	Wattyl Solagard Ultra Premium Low sheen	Taubmans Sunproof Exterior	Accent Solarmax
Self priming on timber[78]	"If painting with white & white tone colours on a tannin rich timber, apply an initial coat of Solagard® as a sealer"[79]	"Tannin rich timbers should be primed with Taubmans Prep Right Wood Primer or Taubmans 3 in 1."[80]	"Where a primer is not specified apply three coats to previously unpainted surfaces"[81]
Table 3. Different priming instructions for acrylic paints.			

But what is the right primer, water, oil or no primer at all? Regardless of the recommendations above, all these manufacturers manufacture a primer suitable for these paints and what are we to make of a comment suggesting a primer may be specified?

A primer is used to provide a strong bond between the wood and succeeding coats. It functions as a sealer and a water repellant, sometimes with fungicides added and is formulated to have a dull finish to aid with the adhesion of the top coats. Timber Queensland are more specific in their advice relating to cladding which is similar to fences in the terms of risk. They say, "For all cladding where a painted finish is required, boards **should** (emphasis mine) be **primed all round** (emphasis mine) with a solvent (oil) based primer plus one coat of undercoat, colour matched to the final finishing coat. This will ensure that significant colour variations will not be apparent due to any shrinkage or movement that may occur later. Knots may be sealed with a two pack polyurethane or other sealer recommended by the paint manufacturer".[82] A primer, most likely oil based, should be part of your paint specification.

What type of paint should you use? In 2006 Timber Queensland advised, "Solvent borne (alkyd or oil) finishes are more resistant to water vapour than water borne (acrylic) finishes. Where a high level of protection is required, a finish system with a solvent borne primer and/or undercoat should be selected". While acknowledging the easier application and the improvements in water based paints, the objection was that "softer films tend to retain more dirt than alkyd (solvent based) paints, and thus harbour more mould growth".[83] Despite advances in paint technology, they saw no reason to revise that recommendation in the March 2014 review of their recommendations. Against this there are now water based enamels that are promising, at least through accelerated weathering trials, to match the performance of the premium acrylics. There can be no substitute for obtaining a written recommendation for a primer and top coat from reputable suppliers especially when new formulations are being released.

A successful painted fence project will include the following:

---

[78] Dulux. *Dulux Weathershield Gloss Datasheet.* URL http://www.duspec.com.au/duspec/file/AUDD0054.pdf. Date accessed. June 16, 2015.

[79] Wattyl. *Wattyl Solagard Ultra Premium Low Sheen. Data Sheet.* URL http://www.wattyl.com.au/export/download/ product_datasheet/D4.14_-_Solagard_Low_Sheen.pdf?pdf. Date accessed. July 16, 2015.

[80] Taubmans. *Sunproof.* URL. http://www.taubmans.com.au/Paints/Sun-Proof. Date accessed. June 16, 2015.

[81] The instructions on the Accents Solarmax can. Date viewed July 17, 2015

[82] Timber Queensland. *Technical Datasheet 5, Cypress and Hardwood Cladding.* (Brisbane: Self Published, 2014), 1. Bootle is less definitive with the term "often used". Bootle, Keith R. *Wood in Australia, Types, properties and uses, Second Edition.* (North Ryde: McGraw Hill Australia, 2005), 151.

[83] Timber Queensland. *Technical Datasheet 2, Finishes for Exterior Timber.* (Brisbane: Self Published, 2014), 1.

- a light colour will be chosen to extend the life of the paint and timber
- housed joints will be sealed
- the ends will be sealed
- the primer will be checked for adhesion if factory applied and
- the top coat will be applied by brush.

Clear Film finishes

A great deal of thought has to be taken before deciding to use clear finishes.. Many professionals have reported very disappointing results to me and a reluctance to use them. This is something I have also observed in many projects and experienced firsthand. Film finishes have to deal with the same variability (as mentioned under the *Paint* section above) which cause many of the problems but not all.

UV Blockers are a critical component of clear film finishes. The finish should contain blockers that protect the timber and different blockers that protect the film itself. These blockers are

Fig. 46. Wall finished with clear film finish, decking with CN oil.

expensive and some low priced finishes have neither! Without the blockers that protect the timber, the fibres start to break down into a fine powder, indiscernible to the naked eye. Once this happens you have a member that is, in effect, wrapped in cling film. The microclimate between the wood and the film can then hasten decay. Any break in the film, which can be caused by natural feature, unsealed butt joints, or fasteners can also allow moisture to enter and promote decay. Leaching of tannin can cause the film to break down from the inside out with hardwoods which is why most clear finish manufacturers recommend a leaching period of something like six to eight weeks. But remember, in our drought prone land, if it has not rained, which it might well not have done over an eight week period, it has not leached so you may have to introduce washing as part of the coating plan. Do not expect recycled timber to be pre-leached. The finish should also be of a thick consistency so forcing the painter to put on a heavy coat.[84]

---

[84] I am aware of one project in North Queensland where the painter applied three thin coats and, after an expensive claim, the manufacturer reformulated the finish so it could not be applied thinly.

Fig. 47. Film finish on fencing.[85]

Fig. 48. Film breaking down after six months

The Achilles heel of film finishes is maintenance. If the film is left to deteriorate it will need to be completely sanded back to bare timber between coats. This means that frequently (if not eventually mostly) recoating simply isn't done. If it is recoated, and it will need to be done on a very regular basis, it will be a costly exercise. These finishes can be used over rough sawn timber but it is necessary to sand before the first coat otherwise a very rough finish results. Manufacturer's recommendations can include a further sand between subsequent coats. Under no circumstances use steel wool to sand as rust marks can develop on the timber.

Penetrating Oils

There is little doubt that the most robust penetrating oil that can be applied is CN oil (refer the decking in Figure Forty-five which is coated in CN Oil). The abbreviation CN stands for copper napthenate. Another positive is that it contains a preservative suitable for a seven year period prior to re-application. Against this superior performance is the unavoidable fact that when it is first applied it looks horrendous. As well, it is not advisable to touch it with your hands when it is still wet. So unfortunately, CN is discounted as a fencing oil. At the time of writing there are no oils other than CN that can be claimed to be a preservative.[86] The main things you can expect from a penetrating oil is that it

Fig. 49. Freshly applied penetrating oil.

works as a water repellant and a UV blocker. The same thing can be said about UV blockers in oils as with clear finishes. They are expensive and some products can have very little of them, indeed they can have very little water repellency as well. Fortunately, unlike paint and clear films, penetrating oils are not affected by dimensional change.[87]

---

[85] This fence is a good example of the use of sawmill recovery sizes.

[86] I was responsible for having one brand which was making this claim reported to the APVMA. If you hear anyone making this claim you need to check it with the APVMA.

[87] Bootle. *Wood...*, 146.

People confuse penetrating oil with film finish as, when the oils are first applied, it does have some level of gloss finish but this is frequently short-lived, especially on unseasoned timber. That does not mean it is not present and not working. Throw water on the surface and you could well find that it is still repelling water. Once the surface stops repelling moisture it is time to re-apply. You do not have to sand back at all. Simply wash off any dust and kill any mould if present and then re-apply oil. This simplicity and relatively low cost makes maintenance a possibility. In many situations, reapplication is not practical and all you can hope for is to apply two or three coats prior to installation and allow the timber to weather to silver grey.

How can you tell a good penetrating oil from one that is less so? Glossy cans and brochures and a high price are not necessarily a reliable guide and marketing claims should not be accepted on face value. Technical data sheets also don't necessarily show the relevant information required to determine a "good quality" product; the saying "oils ain't oils" stands true. A good quality oil should contain ingredients like:

- resin system or oil suitable for timber. Often resins are modified to have characteristics which address limitations of natural oils. This can include mould growth in linseed oil and lanolin.
- UV absorbers which offer protection to timber substrate and resin/oil system.
- water repellents. These can vary significantly in type and quality. It is good to have something that is not prone to mould e.g. again linseed oil and lanolin.
- mould and algae inhibitors. These will not remove or prevent mould from pre-infected timber.
- solvent carrier that aids in penetration of ingredients into timber.

On this last point there are many types of solvent systems. Many penetrating oil formulations contain petroleum based solvents of varying flash points and levels of aromatics as well as those which have surfactants to allow water to be incorporated. The best penetrating oils contain a petroleum based solvent system as it is more able to penetrate into the timber and less prone to facilitate movement of tannins to the surface. A product which incorporates a solvent with a high flashpoint and low aromatics would be preferable. What does this mean? A high flashpoint (>60.5 deg C) will mean the product will not be considered flammable thus reducing risks for transport, storage and use. A low aromatic solvent will reduce odour and risk often associated with using solvents. While these features do not necessarily add to the quality of a product they do provide benefits which make oil based penetrating oils more amenable to use and hence get the best result in timber.[88]

If you are going to apply multiple coats over time those oils containing copper should be avoided as this will tend to blacken the timber.

There is one other very important thing you should expect from a penetrating oil which is critical with CCA treated fencing. That is the ability to seal CCA into the timber and so alleviate any concerns about touching them. I stress that this is more about perceptions than reality. When the APVMA looked closely at CCA and orchestrated its banning in many applications it did not recommend the removal of existing CCA timber structures, including children's playgrounds, and has issued the following

[88] All of these points were considered in the development of Tanacoat. When you are considering specifying a penetrating oil you need to ask probing questions of the manufacturer to ensure you are asking for a product that is at least equal.

statement on painting:

"Will painting arsenic treated timber reduce the risk of arsenic leaching to the surface? Information is limited on the possible benefits of painting treated-timber (including existing structures) to reduce possible risks. Some scientific studies indicate that certain penetrating coatings, such as oil-based semi-transparent stains, when used on a regular basis may reduce the potential for CCA exposure. However, there have been some questions raised about the effectiveness of film-forming or non-penetrating stains because of cracking, peeling and flaking. As such, the APVMA cannot provide any definitive advice at this time on whether there are benefits from painting."[89]

The one thing clear about that statement is that no clear direction is actually given. When Lonza's Tanacoat was developed in conjunction with my former company, Outdoor Structures Australia, we tested its efficacy in sealing CCA to remove any uncertainty. It was very successful. Because of the wide variation in quality in decking oils you should not accept claims of being able to seal in preservatives without evidence.

---

[89] Australian Pesticides and Veterinarian Medicines Authority. The Reconsideration of Registrations of Arsenic Timber Treatment Products (CCA and arsenic trioxide) and Their Associated Labels, Report Of Review Findings And Regulatory Outcomes Summary Report. (Self Published: Canberra. 2005).

12. IMPROVING THE PALING FENCE

Fig. 50. Rails split diagonally in a UK fencing system.

The fences in Figures Forty-nine and Forty-nine show a rail configuration which is not uncommon in the UK and is achieved by splitting a 75x75 diagonally. I have not seen this configuration used in Australia. Generally, whatever Australian timber you are using. they will be prone to bow in this arrangement but it should not be dismissed out of hand as it has the advantage of shedding any moisture and making the fence harder to climb. It also uses 25% less material than a 75x50 rail.

Fig. 51. Close-up showing bent rail and mortise arrangement.

The UK experience is that these rails generally don't bow when in transit if stored horizontally. Presumably they are tightly strapped and cannot move. But "they can warp/bow after being installed if left for a few days before the feather edge close boarding[90] is fixed into position, particularly if the timber is still wet from the treatment process and they're exposed to strong sunlight. They can be straightened by fixing a temporary vertical batten between the rails whilst attaching the close boarding. The middle rail of the centre bay in Figure Fifty shows a rail bowing

---

[90] The term given to what we would call a weatherboard style profile except it is generally only 100 mm wide.

upwards which was rectified in this way."[91] There is probably more application for this profile in the cooler southern states rather than areas where the temperature may be well over 30 degrees Celsius during installation. Invariably, the timber will stay straight if the cladding is secured quickly.

The UK fence shows two important considerations. The first is a preparedness to produce a highly processed post. Modern CNC machines can produce a post trimmed to length, the top profiled and mortices formed in a matter of minutes. The second is the attention to water shedding profiles despite their climate being far more benign to timber than Australia's. Can the principles in this fence be incorporated into one that reflects the Australian climate? I believe so.

Fig. 52. Spotted gum gate in Japan.

Some years ago when exporting spotted gum to Japan, I was asked to develop a fencing system. The brief was to make the system so it could be quickly loaded into a container with a forklift. The standard 4.8m rails did not fit easily into the end of a container. While you can load them it is time consuming and expensive.

A standard Australian fence hides the post behind a wall of palings/pickets but my proposal was to bring the post forward and make it merge into the front of the fence (as in the UK fence above) but to make the post blend into the fence just like another paling/picket. The post would be completely pre-fabricated including the morticing and the rails docked to a convenient length to fit sideways in the container. Fabrication costs became too high. That need not be the case now.[92] The Japanese wholesaler I was dealing with understood the inherent beauty of our hardwoods and that the fencing market should not be one that is used to move low grade product. For their customers, the care taken in selecting quality and attractive material, and the aesthetics of the design reflected upon the home and its owner. Especially as house sites become smaller, you would reasonably expect this attitude to become more common in Australia.

The need to shed moisture from the top of the rail can be accommodated by a 6 mm radius to the top and ideally the bottom as well or a splay. A reversible profile allows the builder the opportunity to keep the best face upwards. It achieves what is illustrated in Figure Forty-nine but avoids the stability issues that can be associated with the split triangular rail in our climate. Using CNC technology there is complete freedom with the design of the tops of the palings and posts allowing custom tops to be produced in a JIT programme.

---

[91] Keighron, Norm. *Pers. Com.* 7 December 2015. Norm is the principal of Keighron Fencing, UK.
[92] A three axis CNC router would produce the post in well under 10 minutes and a paling would take about 20 seconds.

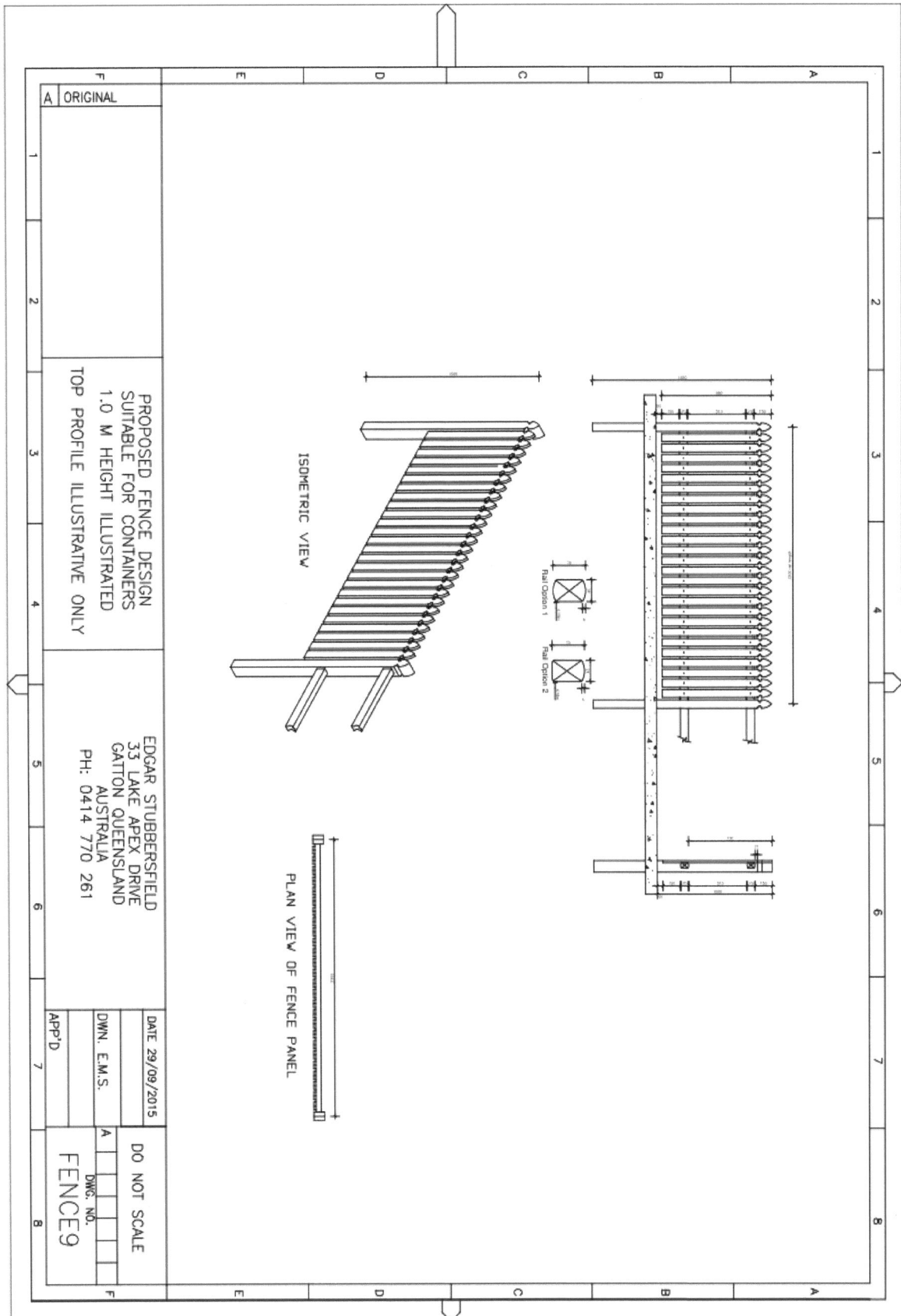

ISOMETRIC VIEW

PLAN VIEW OF FENCE PANEL

Rail Option 1

Rail Option 2

PROPOSED FENCE DESIGN
SUITABLE FOR CONTAINERS
1.0 M HEIGHT ILLUSTRATED

TOP PROFILE ILLUSTRATIVE ONLY

EDGAR STUBBERSFIELD
33 LAKE APEX DRIVE
GATTON QUEENSLAND
AUSTRALIA
PH: 0414 770 261

A ORIGINAL

DATE 29/09/2015

DWN. E.M.S.

APP'D

DO NOT SCALE

DWG. NO.
FENCE9

Fig. 53. Layout of a premium paling/picket fence.

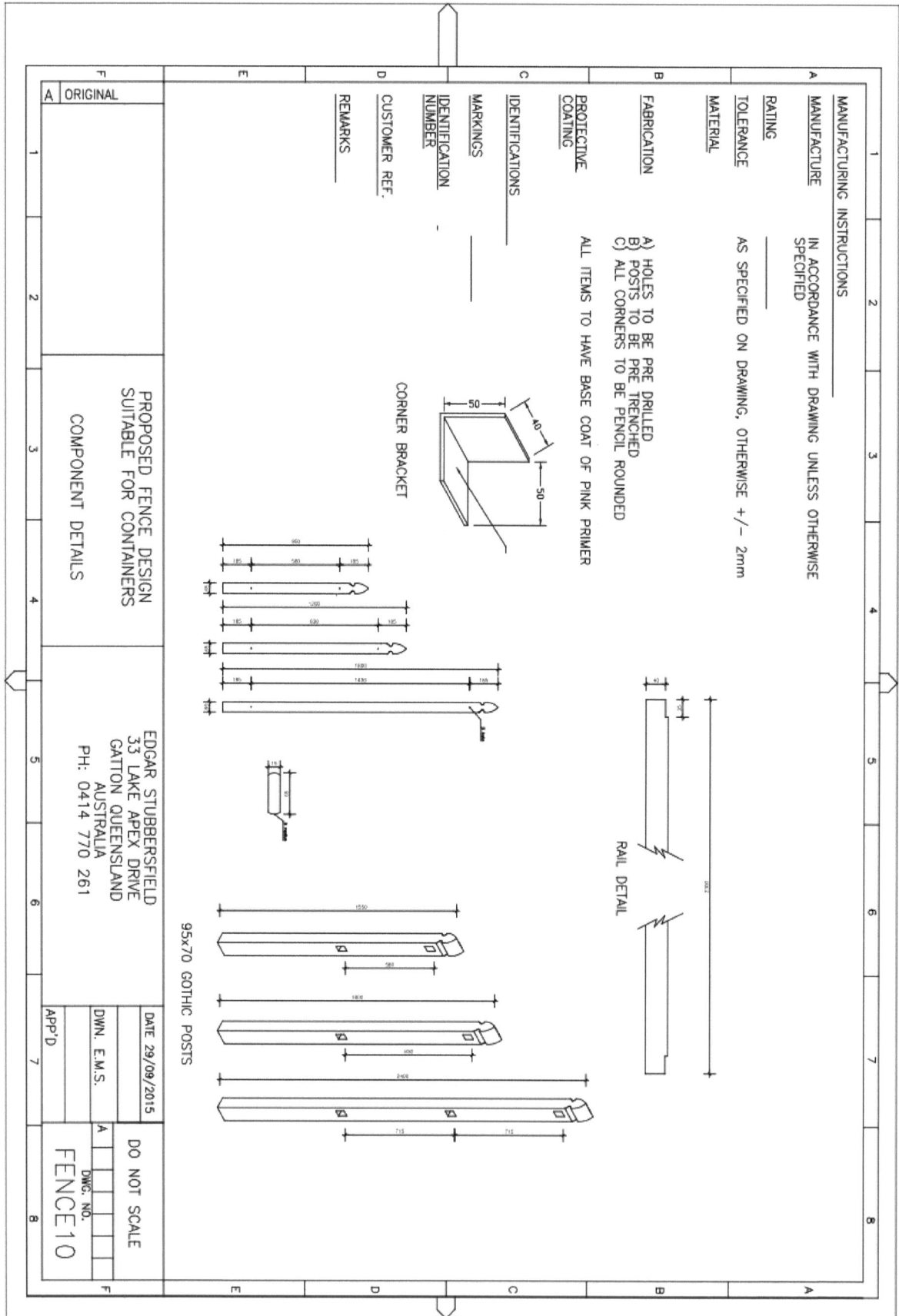

Fig. 54. Components of a premium paling/picket fence.

A fairly simple modification can be made to the unseasoned paling to improve its privacy provision. Once when doing a CPD session, a landscape architect told me how he was facing legal action from one of his clients. He had specified a simple paling fence which was built and then the palings shrunk (as would be expected) which meant there was some loss of privacy and so started the dispute. When asked if there was a solution for the future I proposed what may be called, for lack of a better term, the "privacy paling". The paling is laid tight without a gap as normal and after seasoning they still provide privacy.

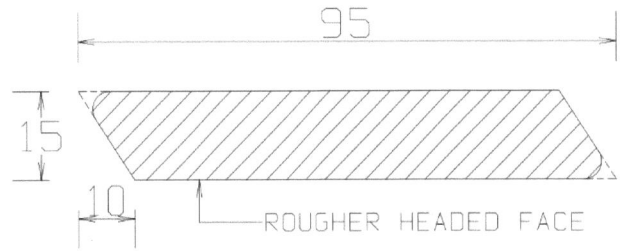

Fig. 55. Privacy paling.

While these two suggested improvements do have merit, the cost driven timber domestic fence market means that it is unlikely that either of these two suggested improvements will see the market any time soon.

13. GATES

Fig.56. Timber entry gates.

The choices in gates and associated hardware are enormous.[93] This is not surprising as a gate can make or break the whole effect of the premises and even the appearance of the most basic treated pine fence can be lifted with decorative hardware.

Fig. 57. Old railway gates at Gatton Historical Society.

The most common problem I have observed with gates over the years is sagging, which can happen a long time before any decay sets in. This is not surprising as gates can be extremely heavy. The timber alone in each gate shown in Figure Fifty-six weighs about 109 kg now that it is dry and would have been 130 kg when installed. Had the builder not lightened the fence by tapering the members in towards the end, each gate would have weighed 158 kg (plus fittings) when installed. But you do not have to look for gates with a 9 metre opening to find gates that have sagged.

Small and relatively inexpensive commercially available gates simply nailed or screwed together can

[93] The search of one "big box" website showed it had almost 600 gate or gate hardware products in its range.

eventually sag. The gates that are frequently offered are simply made of 19 mm softwood decking with a 19 mm softwood top and bottom rail and diagonal brace. The premade timber gates sold in my local "big box' hardware store only had four very small brads at each crossing holding it together. Gates were also available made from 16 mm merbau and screwed together with 8 gauge screws. If you consider that the screw does not protrude, and that the screw itself has a tapered point, once this is taken off the 16 mm, there is only a very short amount of thread holding the rails/brace to the cladding, less than 10 mm. This economy type construction is not advised and instead a solid frame should be built to which the cladding is attached – see Figure Fifty-seven.

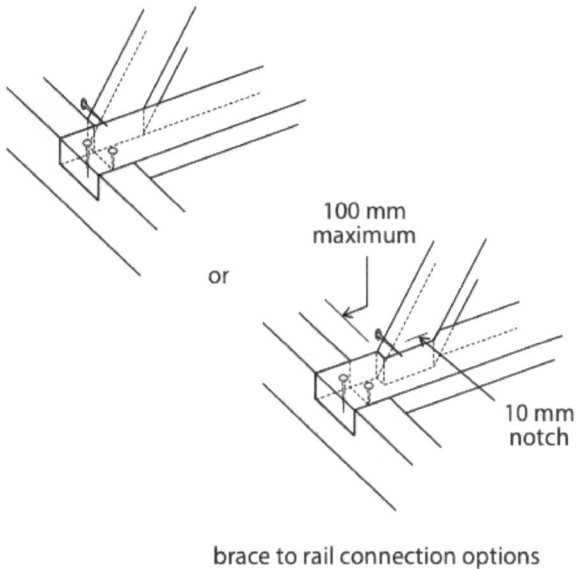

brace to rail connection options

Fig. 58. Gate frame assembly details.

If using housed joints, the timber should be seasoned. Assume that you are building from 70x45 dressed unseasoned spotted gum. The housed joint would be tight when built but after drying the rail will reduce in width giving a 4 mm gap. That means that any advantage you have from a housed joint is soon lost. If unseasoned timber is being used nail plates can achieve a good effect so long as that is supported by closely screwing the plates as well. This is necessary as they are usually pressed out of the timber by the effect of wetting and drying. Proprietary plates are also available which will simplify construction, these should be stainless or in not available painted as per the advice given with steel posts.

The frame for a domestic fence is constructed with the rails of the same size and in the same alignment to the rails of the fence. This would require a three rails for fences larger than 1.2 m. The gate would be hinged at each rail. Fasteners would be either galvanised or stainless depending on the proximity to the ocean.

Screws are to be preferred to bolts whenever possible. Normally, when drilling for a bolt, the hole is 2 mm larger than the thread. As bolts have a rolled thread, the shank is smaller than the thread, giving probably 3 mm movement in the hole. Sagging can then be expected. By contrast, screws are an interference fit.

All hardwood joints should be painted at the time of assembly as the joint will 'bleed" tannin for some after installation and look unsightly.

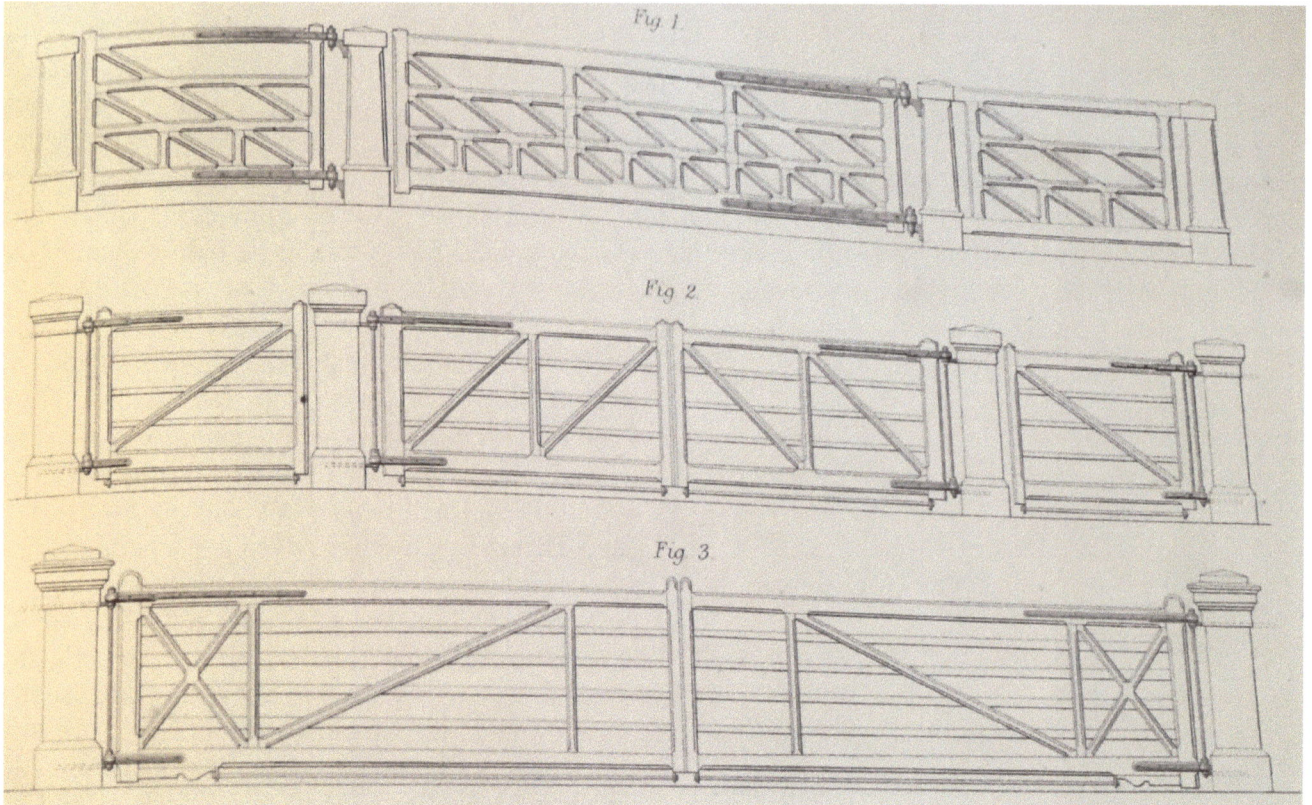

Fig. 59. Designs of UK gates from the 1880's.[94]

The design of the old gates from the UK in Figure Fifty-eight shows how they stopped large gates from sagging. The top hinge has a very long strap, and would appear to be up to 1.5 m long. These are a blacksmith item but well worth considering with expensive custom made timber gates. The brace runs from the latch end of the top rail to the hinge end of the bottom rail meaning that the brace is in compression, where timber works best. Bracing the other direction requires steel which is excellent in tension. The historic gate in Figure Fifty-six combines both timber and steel to their best advantage as the braces.

Gates in Sound Barriers.

Gates in sound barriers have an additional requirement of sealing under the gate but this is not easy to do. Perhaps flexible strips cut from neoprene sheeting would help.

---

[94] Newlands, James. *Carpenters and Joiners Assistant.* (London: Blackie and Son. 1880), 176 and plate LX.

14. CASE HISTORIES

Former Defence Force Housing.

When the Defence Force housing at One Mile (near Amberley Air Force Base, Queensland) was sold to the public, the challenge to the developer was how to make solidly built but uniform fibro and chamfer board houses display some character and individuality. They achieved this very economically by the use of painted timber fences of different standard designs arranged randomly through the community. The outcome was very effective.

Fig. 60. Timber fences, One Mile, Ipswich Queensland.

Kurata Co. Ltd. Shizuoka City, Japan

At the other end of the spectrum to the defence force housing case history is the work of Kurata Co. Ltd in Shizuoka City near Mt Fuji in Japan. The first Shogun, Tokugawa Ieyasu, moved to this town "in his retirement" in 1606 and continued to rule Japan from there until his death in 1616. There, he also built the Sumpo Castle and planned the building of the Edo (Tokyo) Castle. This attracted many of the best timber craftsmen to the area and Shizuoka became famous, and is still to this day, for its timber workmanship. Even now there are regular furniture fairs in the city, where Kurata Co. Ltd. exhibits and promotes Queensland hardwood items and projects.

I have had a long friendship with the Kuratas in Japan and I have been impressed by their totally different approach to fencing. We have spoken many times and shared what we both had learnt specialising in weather exposed spotted gum, but I could never aspire to the craftsmanship they regularly bring to their projects. It is hardly surprising as they started as furniture manufacturers in a marketplace that would accept nothing less than excellence. In a sense, since 1995, they are have been manufacturing exterior furniture.

Fig. 61. Curved timber fence rail, domestic project. Shizuoka City, Japan.

Fig. 62. Different views of residential fence.

In the Chapter on improving the paling fence I spoke about the possibility of using CNC technology for producing higher quality fencing with a much larger range of possibilities. Kurata Co Ltd. have done just that. By using their CNC capability, they are not constrained by the inflexibility of straight lines or the high cost of working "specials" by hand.

Residential Estate, Laidley.

The residential estate in Laidley, Queensland, (shown in Figure Sixty-two), is the other end of the spectrum to the fencing supplied by Kurata Co. Driving past, it looks like any pine fence but stop and look closely it is clear that it could have been much better. The fencing uses hardwood posts coupled to pine rails and palings and this can provide an acceptable fence. A number of different contractors were involved as the fences were built as the housing was constructed so there is variability in its construction quality between lots. The project demonstrates the need, even in low cost fencing, to have some standards. Are these fences any worse than the average estate fencing? Probably not. This development is about two minutes away from one of hardwood sawmills I mentioned previously that knew what would be required for satisfactory performance and supplied material suitable for the application. Incidentally, when the quality awards for sawmills were operation in Queensland we would take it in turns with this mill for first prize and runner up.

Fig. 63. General view of the residential estate.

Fig. 64. Screws withdrawing from post.

Fig. 65. Defect full width of two sides.

In the chapter *Timber Species and Quality,* I advised having a specification for the timber instead of just a dimension. Figure Sixty-three shows a rail with a single batten screw which has pulled away from the post as it was installed into an unsound knot. Figure Sixty-four shows a post that has a defect so large that it completely covers two sides and is then installed with the defect at groundline. While still not best practice, simply end for ending the post would have been much better. All posts are set in concrete. On the positive side, the posts weren't notched.

Fig. 66. Marrying in later fence to existing.

Fig. 67. Rails nailed to posts.

There were differences in construction between the different runs when it came to attaching the rails. Figure Sixty-four shows a single batten screw being used but in Figure Sixty-six we see another contractor has just nailed on the rails which easily detached. In Figure Sixty-five, the contractor had to marry a new fence in with an existing fence. What looks like scraps of untreated pine from a piece of furniture were nailed to the existing fence and the new rails nailed into the end grain of the old furniture. For some reason the rail was not put in the centre between the top and bottom rail and the movement of the palings was excessive. The nails were the industry recommended 45x2.5 mm galvanised ring shank but the movement in many palings would suggest to me that a bigger nail would have seen better results.

Fig. 68. Little thought in construction.

Fig. 69. Only one centre nail.

The level of care in construction at places was very poor, as illustrated by Figure Sixty-seven. Most palings only had one nail at the centre rail allowing many of the palings to move. Where two central nails were used the palings remained straighter. In some areas there was little care in the placement of the nails and they could be very near the edge. In fact I found one paling that had two central nails, one missed the top of the rail and the other missed the bottom!

Considering what could have been constructed, it makes what we see in this case history the more frustrating. But while much better quality material was available, it means little if construction practices do not match.

SOURCE OF IMAGES

Where copyright is not acknowledged, ownership is with the author

	Cover image	Aki Kurata, Kurata Co. Ltd.
1	Fence more than a boundary	Colin McKenzie
3	Japanese traffic barrier	Ken Thompson, Matrol marketing
11	Cypress fencing	Colin McKenzie
12	Posts with heart	Graeme Lavuschewski, Westside Timbers
13	Corrosion at groundline	Ralph Bailey, Guymer Bailey Architects
27	Japanese fence	Aki Kurata, Kurata Co. Ltd.
28	Subdivision fence	Dennis Clark Photography
31	Water shedding profile	Dennis Clark Photography
32	Diagonal top rail	Dennis Clark Photography
33	Protruding bolt	Dennis Clark Photography
34	Bollard by author	Dennis Clark Photography
35	Bollard by others	Dennis Clark Photography
41	Plywood fence	Shaun Egan, Place Design Group
44	Fencing brackets	Dennis Clark Photography
45	Painted fence	Kerry Murray, Fencescape Fencing Pty. Ltd
46	Wall with clear film finish	Tom Lenigas
50	UK Fence	Keighron Fencing Ltd.
51	UK Fence with bent rail	Keighron Fencing Ltd.
52	Japanese gate	Aki Kurata, Kurata Co. Ltd.
56	Gate image	Richard Travers, Allkind Joinery and Glass
58	Gate frame detail	Timber Queensland
61	Japanese fence	Aki Kurata, Kurata Co. Ltd.
62	Japanese fence	Aki Kurata, Kurata Co. Ltd.

WORKS CITED

Australian Pesticides and Veterinarian medicines Authority. *The Reconsideration of Registrations of Arsenic Timber Treatment Products (CCA and arsenic trioxide) and Their Associated Labels, Report Of Review Findings And Regulatory Outcomes Summary Report.* (Self Published: Canberra. 2005).

Bootle, Keith R. *Wood in Australia, Types, properties and uses, Second Edition.* (North Ryde: McGraw Hill Australia, 2005).

Carter Holt Harvey. *Ironwood Landscaping.* http://www.chhwoodproducts.com.au/ironwood landscaping/ Date visited. 8 October 2015.

Carter Holt Harvey. *Shadowclad Installation Guide, March 2014.* (CHH. No publication details)

John Lysaght (Australia) Limited. *Lysaght Referee* 27th Edition. (Sydney: John Lysaght. 1985)

Newlands, James. *Carpenters and Joiners Assistant.* (London: Blackie and Son. 1880).

New Zealand Transport Agency. *State Highway Noise Barrier Design Guide, Version 1.0.* (Self published. 2010),

One Steel Trading. *Duragal Flooring System – Issue 6.* No publication details

Plywood Association of Australia. *Facts About Plywood – 2012 Edition.* (PAA. No publication details)

Plywood Association of Australia. *Featuring Plywood in Buildings, Revision 5.* (PAA. No publication Details)

Plywood Association of Australia. *Product and Specification Guide for the Professional and Home Handyperson.* (PAA, No publication details).

Roads and Traffic Authority. *Noise Wall Design Guidelines.* (RTA: 2007).

Standards Australia. *AS2082-2010 Visually stress-graded hardwood for structural purposes.* (Standards Australia: Homebush, 2010).

Timber Advisory Service. *Timber Fences.* (Surry Hills: Self published, 2003).

Timber Queensland. *Technical Datasheet 2, Finishes for Exterior Timber.* (Brisbane: Self Published, 2014).

Timber Queensland. *Technical Datasheet 4, Residential Timber Decks*. (Brisbane: Self Published, 2014).

Timber Queensland *Technical Datasheet 5, Cypress and Hardwood Cladding*. (Brisbane: Self Published, 2014).

Timber Queensland. *Technical Data Sheet 9 Timber Retaining Walls*. (Brisbane: Timber Queensland. 2014)

Timber Queensland. *Technical Data Sheet 20 Residential Timber Fences*. (Brisbane: Timber Queensland. 2014)

Vicroads. *A Guide to the Reduction of Traffic Noise,* (Vicroads. 1994, reprinted 2003).

ABOUT THE AUTHOR

Ted Stubbersfield was born in the small Queensland town of Gatton in 1950. After studying to be a pastor in Brisbane and the UK he returned to the family business, Gatton Sawmilling Co. A fair question would be, "Can anything good come out of Gatton"? Well, Gatton was the home of a Governor General of Australia (William Vanneck 1938). It is also the home of the best and most innovative hardwood producer in Australia, Outdoor Structures Australia (OSA).

The family had been involved in sawmilling and building for about 140 years and a lot of knowledge has passed through the generations. In 1985 we ventured into the footbridge market (almost by accident) and then followed public landscaping. Initially, we just did as we were told by consultants who knew very little about timber. In about 1988 Ted decided he would come to know the medium he was working with far better than any of his competitors and most of the professionals who used his products.

Ted realised that there were no useful standards and guides for designing and building weather exposed timber structures such as boardwalks. That led in 1997 to his first formal research project on boardwalk design, engineering supply and construction. Over the years there followed a complete set of guides. These allowed professionals to design timber structures of exceptional beauty and durability. Typically, everybody wants to re-invent the wheel and the guides were usually ignored. Invariably, the same mistakes keep being made over and over. This little book is an attempt to remedy this.

In 2012, the time came to close the manufacturing arm of OSA and to take on a less stressful lifestyle. Ted plans to put in writing much of what he has learnt so the industry does not have to relearn it. This book on timber fences is the ninth in a series of Timber Design Files that are intended to show designers how to avoid the pitfalls of common, but often bad practice as well as Standards that can be very inadequate and engender a false sense of security. In the case of timber fencing, of course, there is no standard.

www.ingramcontent.com/pod-product-compliance
Lightning Source LLC
Chambersburg PA
CBHW060802270326
41926CB00002B/65